STEAL THIS BOOK, NOT MY VOTE

Handbook for the Wisconsin Nonviolent Revolution

Barbara With

Mad Island Communications
La Pointe, WI

STEAL THIS BOOK, NOT MY VOTE

Handbook for the Wisconsin Nonviolent Revolution

ISBN 978-0-9661378-2-8

Editors: Rebecca Kemble, Barbara Daughter
Contributers: Rebecca Kemble, Michael Matheson,
Brenda Konkel, Grant Petty, Sheila Parks
Editorial Assistance: Peg Randall Gardner, Carolyn Moon,
Bernie Schlafke, Murial Krugman, Robin Posekany

Please pass this book on to all good Americans who wish to protect the Bill of Rights and the Constitution, and understands the gravity of the current situation.

We will not rest until we have achieved the goal of
SECURE HAND COUNT PAPER BALLOT ELECTIONS,
open and transparent for all to observe
that our votes are safe.

Recount photos courtesy of
Wisconsin Citizens for Election Protection
and Wisconsin Counts!

go to www.barbarawith.com/footnotes.html for
online access to the footnotes

Mad Island Communications
P.O. Box 153
La Pointe, WI 54850
715.209.5471
www.barbarawith.com

ACKNOWLEDGMENTS

Thanks to Abbie Hoffman and his classic *Steal This Book,* published in 1977 as a handbook for the rebellion of those times. While we share the same dogged dedication to dissent, civic duty and using one's voice to educate and inspire action, our ways part in that I am an advocate for nonviolence.

This work could not have been completed without the wisdom, dedication and guidance of all the Election Integrity leaders who came before me, including Brad Friedman, Bob Fitrakis, Jeannie Dean, the Colliers—Victoria, Jim, Kenneth and Phyllis, Richard Charnin, Bev Harris, Sheila Parks, John Washburn, Jonathan Simon, Sally Castleman, Nirtana Goodman, and all the others who watched the Supreme Court steal the election for George W. Bush in 2000 and have not slept well since. To Mary Magnuson, Jean Perron, Darcy Gustavsson and all the other observers at the Kloppenburg-Prosser recount who came forward, and every other good citizen of Wisconsin who has been standing up in nonviolent protest against the assault to steal our votes, for teaching me how much power we really have.

Many deep, personal thanks go to Marianne Moonhouse, Jim Mueller, Katy Reeder, and Sue Trace for the breath-taking leadership in the line of duty after the 2011 Wisconsin Supreme Court recount. Upon realizing the recalls were in danger, you led the way to germinate the first blooms of an installation of election protection in a way no one had accomplished before you.

Huge gratitude goes to Joseph Skulan, Rebecca Kemble, Mike Wiggins Jr., Jason and Cherie Pero, the Bad River and Red Cliff Bands of the Lake Superior Tribe of Chippewa Indians and all the sovereign nations of Wisconsin, Nicole Desautels Schulte, Jason Huberty, Craig, Emma & Jack Spaulding, Edward Kuharski, Linda Hedenblad, Jenna Pope, Peg Randall Gardner, Carolyn Moon, Bernie Schlafke, Bart Munger, Robin Posekany, Joanie Sedarski, Paul Demain, Blue Cheddar, Segway Jeremy Ryan, Arthur Kohl-Riggs, Lisa Wells, Janet Jesberger, Bill Dunn, Samantha Masterton, Leslie Amsterdam, Frank Koehn, Sarah Martinez, Charles Ortman, Pete Rasmussen, Thi Le, The Terrells, Sarah LittleRedFeather Kalmanson, Kimberly Sprecher, Dorothy Kegley, Brandon Barwick, Dennis Kern, Beverly Jean Skelton, Dorothy Mickleburgh, Stephanie Leigh, Prentice H. Berge, Daithi Wolf, Lance Link, Paul Schmid, Tim Riley, Roberta Retrum, Laura Chern, Jen Miller, Sierra Nolan, Michael Matheson, Nick Nice, Melanie Kondziella, Genie Ogden, Capper, Kelley Albrecht, Ryan Wherley, Valerie van Horn, Mary Jo Walters, Whitney and Kathy Steffen, Joanne Swartzberg, Pizza Box Man and Will, Karen Tuerk, Todd Endres, Gwen Carr, Jean Sielaff, Jeri Jafek, Barb and Larry Truitt, Tom and Pam Robson, Miles Kristan, Chris Reeder and the Solidarity Sing Along, Lane Hall, Lisa Moline and the Overpass Light Brigade, and everyone else I did not mention who continue to put your bodies on the front line to withstand the slings and arrows of this corporate attack. It's an honor to be still standing with you loud and proud and strong. You are all heroes to me.

Last but not least, to Madeline Island, Lake Superior, the Penokee Hills and all of Wisconsin's well-preserved and long-cherished natural resources. Long may we stand.

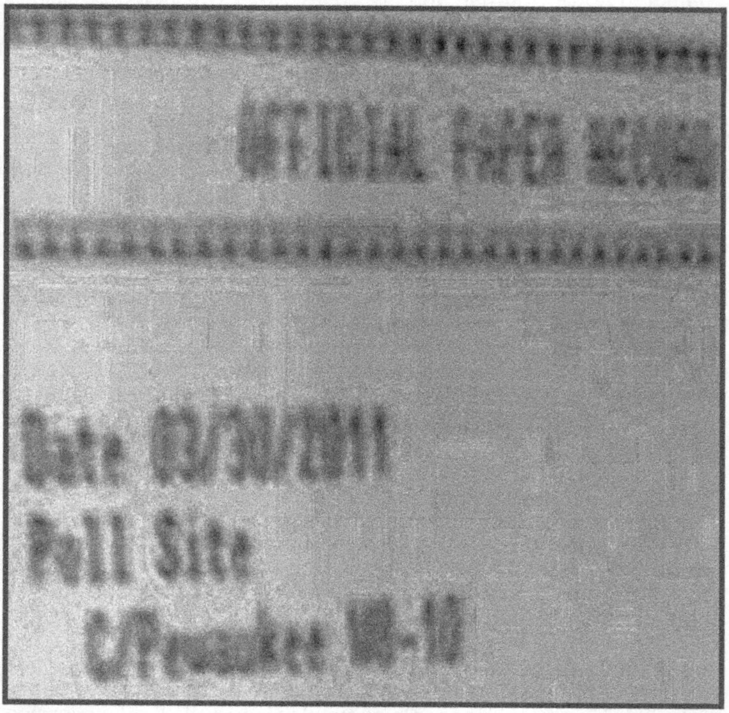

One of several photos of a touchscreen poll tape I observed Friday, May 16, 2011 at the Supreme Court recount from the City of Pewaukee. Dated March 30, 2011 1:40 AM for an election that took place April 5, 2011, election official Barbara Hanson, overseeing the recount in Waukesha, confirmed twice that this was an official ballot. Another clerk was also sworn in and testified that this was indeed a real ballot, that the votes were taken on April 5, 2011, but that she could not confirm how they got to be dated March 30.

After this poll tape was discovered on Friday, the recount schedule for the following Monday changed. Observers were told to stay away until after lunch because the board had some "paperwork to catch up on." I arrived at the courthouse at noon to find all the poll workers finishing lunch together.

At that session, I submitted a written request to the canvassing board to include in the minutes a feasible explanation for how this mistaken date stamping occurred. It was then I was told there "were no touch screen votes from Pewaukee."

Subsequent investigation with voting machine representative Aaron Storbeck confirmed that the only way to get an official ballot dated five days before an election is to insert the programmed pac designed to be used on election day into the voting machine on March 30 and run off votes. It could not be due to the machine's batteries being low. Voting machines are powered by chords and their batteries are seldom used. When they do run down, a large yellow band flashes across the bottom of the screen indicating the clerk is to call the vendor for service.

TABLE OF CONTENTS

Declaration of Independence

When in the Course of human events, it becomes necessary for one people to dissolve the political bands which have connected them with another, and to assume among the powers of the earth, the separate and equal station to which the Laws of Nature and of Nature's God entitle them, a decent respect to the opinions of mankind requires that they should declare the causes which impel them to the separation.

We hold these truths to be self-evident, that all men are created equal, that they are endowed by their Creator with certain unalienable Rights, that among these are Life, Liberty, and the pursuit of Happiness -- That to secure these rights, Governments are instituted among Men, deriving their just powers from the consent of the governed -- That whenever any Form of Government becomes destructive of these ends, it is the Right of the People to alter or abolish it, and to institute new Government, laying its foundation on such principles, and organizing its powers in such form, as to them shall seem most likely to affect their Safety and Happiness.

Prudence, indeed, will dictate that Governments long established should not be changed for light and transient causes; and accordingly all experience hath shewn, that mankind are more disposed to suffer, while evils are sufferable, than to right themselves by abolishing the forms to which they are accustomed. But when a long train of abuses and usurpations, pursuing invariably the same Object, evinces a design to reduce them under absolute Despotism, it is their right, it is their duty, to throw off such Government, and to provide new Guards for their future security.

Such has been the patient sufferance of these Colonies; and such is now the necessity which constrains them to alter their former Systems of Government. The History of the present King of Great Britain is a history of repeated injuries and usurpations, all having in direct object the establishment of an absolute Tyranny over these States. To prove this, let Facts be submitted to a candid world.

July 4 1776

waukesha_county_recount_minutes_all_pdf_74466.pdf

Name of Municipality: **City of Pewaukee**

Reporting Unit: Wards 8 - 10

Electronic Voting Equipment Test Results: Not applicable to this Reporting Unit.

Number of Voters from Registration List: 1,568

Number of Absentee Ballot Applications: 144

Number of Probable Absentee Ballots Identified by the Tabulators: 147

Despite my letter submitted to the recount canvas board on Monday, May 19, 2011 at the Waukesha County Courthouse asking that they include in the minutes a feasible explanation for how this mistaken date stamping occurred, none were. This is the entry from the official recount minutes for the City of Pewaukee, wards 8-10, the very tape above dated March 30, 2011, 1:40 AM.

"Electronic voting equipment test results: Not applicable to this Reporting Unit."

DEFINITION OF ELECTION FRAUD

- ✓ **Election fraud** is not just corrupted officials "finding" 14,000 votes two days after an election;
- ✓ It's not just voting machines that can be rigged with no discernible trace and proven by Princeton University to be hackable;
- ✓ It's not just gerrymandering by redistricting using $395-an-hour attorneys at taxpayer cost to draw up secret maps and making legislators sign secrecy agreements to diminish democratic representation;
- ✓ It's not just disenfranchising and intimidating students;
- ✓ It's not just phone calls saying that people do not need to vote if they already signed the petition for the recall;
- ✓ It's not just exit polling not 'matching' the previous exit polling minutes before;
- ✓ It's not just the Central Tabulator that controls votes remotely;
- ✓ It's not just a voter suppression law that outright keeps voters from the polls and was rammed through the legislature only to later be declared unconstitutional;
- ✓ It's not just Election Day confusion because of closed polling places, misinforming the public, providing clerks with confusing information and running out of ballots;
- ✓ It's not just threatening to close DMVs where IDs can be obtained in Democratic districts;
- ✓ It's not just Americans for Prosperity sending out absentee ballot application forms to Democrats with erroneous information meant to mislead;
- ✓ It's not just propaganda that makes people believe the state has turned right-wing to "balance the budget";
- ✓ It's not just a right-wing "ALEC"-type organization named "Election Center," the brainchild of the voting machine companies and now a staple for election officials who support the corruptible voting machines;
- ✓ It's not just a Government "Accountability" Board whose staff censors information getting to board members;
- ✓ It's not just voting machine distributor Command Central giving out two free touchscreens to wards all across the State;
- ✓ It's not just Democrats who concede elections before all the votes are counted and don't demand justice;

It's all this and more, and Wisconsin has verifiable proof that election fraud is alive and functioning in this state.

HOW TO USE THIS BOOK

In the summer of 2011 I filed a Racketeer Influenced and Corrupt Organization (RICO) complaint with the Department of Justice concerning what was happening in Wisconsin, which appeared to be the beginning of the hostile takeover of our government. This book is the result of several people urging me to publish the complaint. The editorial views put forth here are based on eye-witness experiences and investigations, presented as an anecdotal account of living through the events.

I never set out to be a reporter. But the circumstances in Wisconsin are calling for everyone to stand up to protect our Democracy before it's wrestled away completely by the corporate thieves who are raiding our State. As a writer and publisher by trade, I felt compelled to contribute my skills to document events and move information. To that end, this is also a history book, as much of the story behind the story as I know.

I also wish to suggest pro-active steps to stand up to a takeover of the government, but this is not an easy task. Decidedly, absorbing the scope of this US fascism, and the systematic election fraud and its momentum to date makes it a difficult issue to face—but all the evidence is there for anyone who cares to look for it. Still, there are no easy answers. But people must ***learn for themselves*** what is happening, then understand and process the *shock and awe*. Independent, critical thinking is the first step to getting over the shock, which then can lead to action. We need all hands on deck to protect our rights. Unfortunately non-participatory Democracy is no longer an option.

We must learn to speak the truth everywhere we go. We must not be afraid to sit down with family and friends and have specific conversations about the story behind the story. We must demand of our legislators, judges and all elected officials in no uncertain terms: "As my public servant, you either stand up and take action to protect our rights, including fair and open elections, or you will be considered a traitor to the US Constitution and the oath you swore to protect us. When you make laws that strip us of our rights and keep control in the hands of voting machine vendors and their corporate allies, you commit treason."

I am adding my voice to the growing sentiment: demand paper ballots be used in fair, transparent and hand-counted elections. They do it all over the world. Nothing short will suffice.

I also encourage you to file your own complaint with the Department of Justice. Please copy any of the language in this book. Use it to create a *Handbook For the Nonviolent Revolution* specific to your state.

Restoring Democracy begins with election reform. Time to rein in and hold accountable those politicians from all parties making oaths and demonstrating allegiance to organizations, individuals or ideologies other than the State and US Constitutions and protecting the people. No matter what these traitors say or how they act, they are our public servants, not our masters. When they steal our votes, they steal our voices, and then they steal our power.

Time to get alpha-dog! Without hyperbole, I tell you that the survival of our Republic depends on it.

Barbara With
Ft. La Pointe, Fitzwalkerstan[1]

1 *Fitzwalkerstan*: a nickname for Wisconsin coined by Rep. Mark Pocan (D-WI), February 2011, based on Scott Walker, Sen. Scott Fitzgerald (R), Assemblyman Jeff Fitzgerald (R) and their father, Stephen Fitzgerald, head of Wisconsin State Troopers.

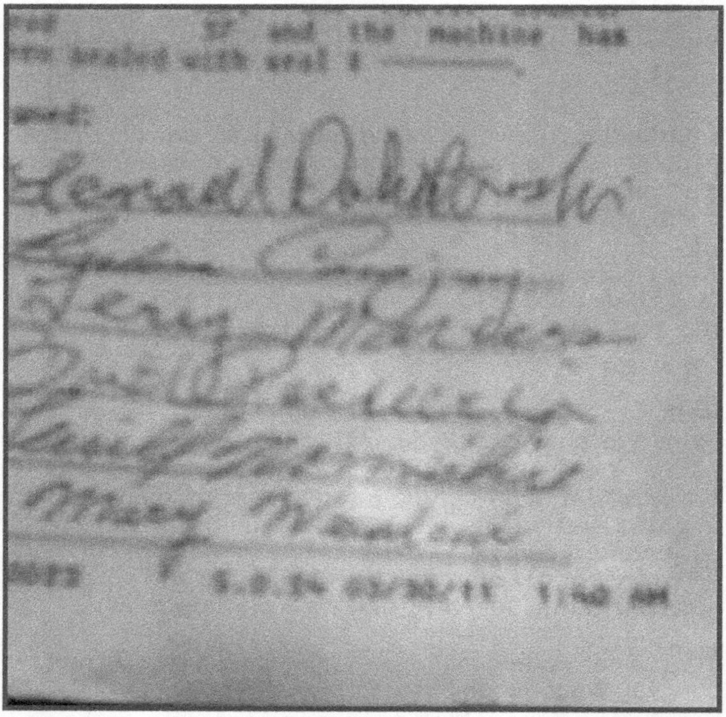

Another view of the touch screen poll tape from Pewaukee dated March 30, 2011 1:40 AM for an election that took place April 5, 2011. Did all the clerks sign on that date and at that time? Were they asked to sign afterward since, according to the voting machine vendor who services these kinds of machines, there is no feasible way this happened short of running the votes on March 30?

Voting machines require two programming pacs: one used a week before the elections to test the machines, and another used on Election Day. Since the tests are made with a different programming pac, if this were a test tape it would have PLAT TEST across the top, not OFFICIAL BALLOT.

So when was this tape printed and whose votes are they?

"Forward" by Jean P. Miner, Wisconsin State Capitol

FORWARD!

I was part of a group of observers at the April 2011 recount of the Wisconsin Supreme Court Prosser/Kloppenburg election. We observed as copious evidence of election fraud was ignored and votes that should have been disqualified were counted for Republican David L. Prosser, who despite a documented history of partisan legal infractions, was waved onto the bench. His duplicitous victory came just in time, as he immediately overturned a lower court's ruling that the Republicans had violated Open Meetings Law in March when they illegally tried to strip the collective bargaining rights of Wisconsin public workers in the middle of the night, locking out the public.

STEAL THIS BOOK, NOT MY VOTE is my eyewitness account from the front lines of the Wisconsin revolution beginning February 2011. After the Democrats left the state, I established an online presence to report daily as a citizen journalist on Facebook and eventually became a founding member of Wisconsin Citizen Media Coop (wcmcoop.com). Throughout 2011-2012, I listened live to hours of legislative debates and committee meetings, as well as to the very trial that Prosser overturned.

Along with my participation at the recount, I testified about the results at the Committee on Election Reform in June 2011. After seeing the election fraud firsthand, I filed a formal complaint with and testified at the Government Accountability Board meeting, which led to uncovering possible suppression of evidence on the part of the staff.[1] I assisted recount volunteers in establishing Wisconsin Citizens for Election Protection and supported the implementation of an outreach program to bring reform. Along the way, I interviewed a voting machine vendor from Command Central at the County Clerks Association meeting in Ladysmith in June 2011 and obtained evidence of misrepresentation on their part. After investigating activities of the voting machine vendors, I filed a RICO Complaint with the Department of Justice. Along with other members of Wisconsin Citizens Media Coop, we also helped stop AB426, a mining bill written by a mining company, through testifying, educating others and speaking up.

Since Scott Walker took office in January 2011, Wisconsin has been under attack by corporate politicians who seem to be engaged in a hostile takeover of our government. This takeover appears to be a well-executed, long-term plan to destroy our republic and turn America's resources, state by state, over to the ALEC/Rove/Koch/Cline et al corporate cartel to wage endless war upon the world. Through systemic election rigging, they have placed corrupt politicians and court justices in power to change the laws, dismantle both the State and Federal Constitutions, with the ultimate goal of a society that reflects the corporate cartel's personal vision. We the People will become the expendable labor force used to feed a perpetual war-making machine, advanced by passing legislation designed to strip us of our rights, put our water, air and land at risk, lay economic siege to our communities, and take complete control of our governance.

My participation on the frontline barricades in Wisconsin since February 2011 made me realize that even people living in our state had no idea what was going on. Between the media's shameful lack of investigative reporting and the propaganda machine working overtime to spin the corporatist

---

1 August 2011 GAB meeting revealed the Board was not informed of the evidence that surfaced at the recount before deciding Prosser won. Director Kevin Kennedy admitted in an e-mail that the staff has the power to withhold information from the Board, including not passing my complaint against Waukesha County Clerk Kathy Nickolaus and Kennedy himself on to the Board until after the election was called.

agenda, there is nothing left here of our Fourth Estate. The press is mainly corporate-driven and part of the fraud being perpetrated. The real stories—the criminal acts on the part of legislators, the shutting down of open government, the police state Walker has installed in Wisconsin—aren't being reported. To get those, you need to go into the legislature and watch your government in action. Social media is vital, but it is literally in the streets is where you find the honest truth. The upshot is that here in Wisconsin we've experienced corruption so deep and wide at the highest offices, one might think there is no solution.

However, I believe this is the very catalyst Americans need to finally turn off the TV and become more directly involved in a robust and vigorous participation in our Democracy. In fact, I believe we have no other choice than to take action or we will lose this great Republic to the slavery experienced today in so many other parts of the world.

Pondering what I could contribute, I decided to write and publish *STEAL THIS BOOK, NOT MY VOTE* to help others understand how we got here, provide overall context so you can connect the dots for yourself and share what others in Wisconsin are doing to stand up to protect our state. My hope is to help move us beyond the *shock and awe*, suggest clear action steps to protect our rights and restore justice, and then inspire you to take those steps.

Since I started this book in July 2011, the Occupy Wall Street movement has risen all across the world as nonviolent resistance manifested in the hearts of people everywhere to demand an end to all wars and discover new ways to bring social, economic, political and environmental justice. Wisconsin has often been cited as the "Mother of the Occupy Movement" due to the occupation of the capitol in Madison by the citizens of this state in February 2011, week after week in the dead of winter. Hope rises when we see ordinary people, members of what are now called the 99%, standing up to protect their rights.

In order to form a more perfect union, I am convinced we must force fair, open and transparent elections. We need every American citizen standing up and taking action to protect his or her vote ... but we must start **now.**

I believe that the citizen movement that arose in Wisconsin during that messy, irreconcilable Supreme Court recount is America's last great hope: *Election Protection.* Birthed in the US in the 1970s—when James and Kenneth Collier discovered corrupted vote counts from Miami-Dade County machines in the Florida state congressional race—and since carried on through the decades by brave activists all over the country, election reform will change the course of the corporate takeover of our country.

No system can survive with an infrastructure built on falsehoods, constructed to support the few at the expense of the many. Repeating lies that claim otherwise won't make them true. Our survival desperately depends on good citizens educating themselves and then lifting their voices to speak the truth and demand change.

Here in Wisconsin, we have a deep and unshakable tradition that goes back generations—we instinctively create systems that serve the greater good to benefit all. It's why we're such an extraordinary state and why, I believe, we were given this place in history. It's also why the fraud and deceit have been exposed so easily: By our nature, Wisconsinites play fair and work together.

Scott Walker and the state Republicans, mimicking the national tone of bullying, fear and lies, are standing out like Bear fans at Lambeau Field. Their legislation is passed without real debate—*lock-step extortion-voting* for the good of the corporate sponsors who are buying them their votes. As more and more citizens wake to this truth, more and more are rising up to take action.

Thanks to our deep-seated sense of peace and justice, and glorious history of leading national reform, Wisconsin stands ready for the task of exposing these traitors once and for all, and holding them accountable for their crimes.

Wisconsin is intuitively constructive. There is no lack of creative vision on how to restructure government to protect our rights and prevent this from happening again. If anyone can build new, regenerative community-sustaining systems inclusive of all in our society, but especially for the environment and those in need, it's Wisconsin.

In August 2011, after watching Wisconsin being assaulted from all sides by election, legislative, media and judicial fraud, I filed a complaint with the US Department of Justice.

Since election fraud was just a piece of the puzzle, I asked the Department of Justice to consider my rationale for RICO: the Racketeer Influenced and Corrupt Organizations Act, the only legal action that could encompass the entire scope of the long-term assault we are under. The Defendants include Scott Walker, Karl Rove, The Kochs, and the American Legislative Exchange Council (ALEC), to name a few.

The hubris and propaganda of the Defendants will be their undoing. We the People must be ready to build a new foundation based on what is best for the good of all. Once again, Wisconsin stands poised to be called to service as a reformer for America.

To the citizens of Wisconsin, I say: This is not about left or right; it's about right and wrong. It's about participation in justice. Republican, Democrat, Independent, Green—if you do not act to help bring election reform, you will essentially allow them to steal your vote. What will it take to get you to take action?

To the corporate vote-buyers, I say: Sorry, you picked the wrong state to mess with. The corporatocracy's rape and destruction of our planet ends here in Wisconsin. And if anyone can stop the collusion of these big money-humping miners, corporate lackeys, patsy politicians, phat-cat lobbyists and other arrogant high-ranking offenders and set these yahoos back on their well-oiled heels—it's us.

Game on.

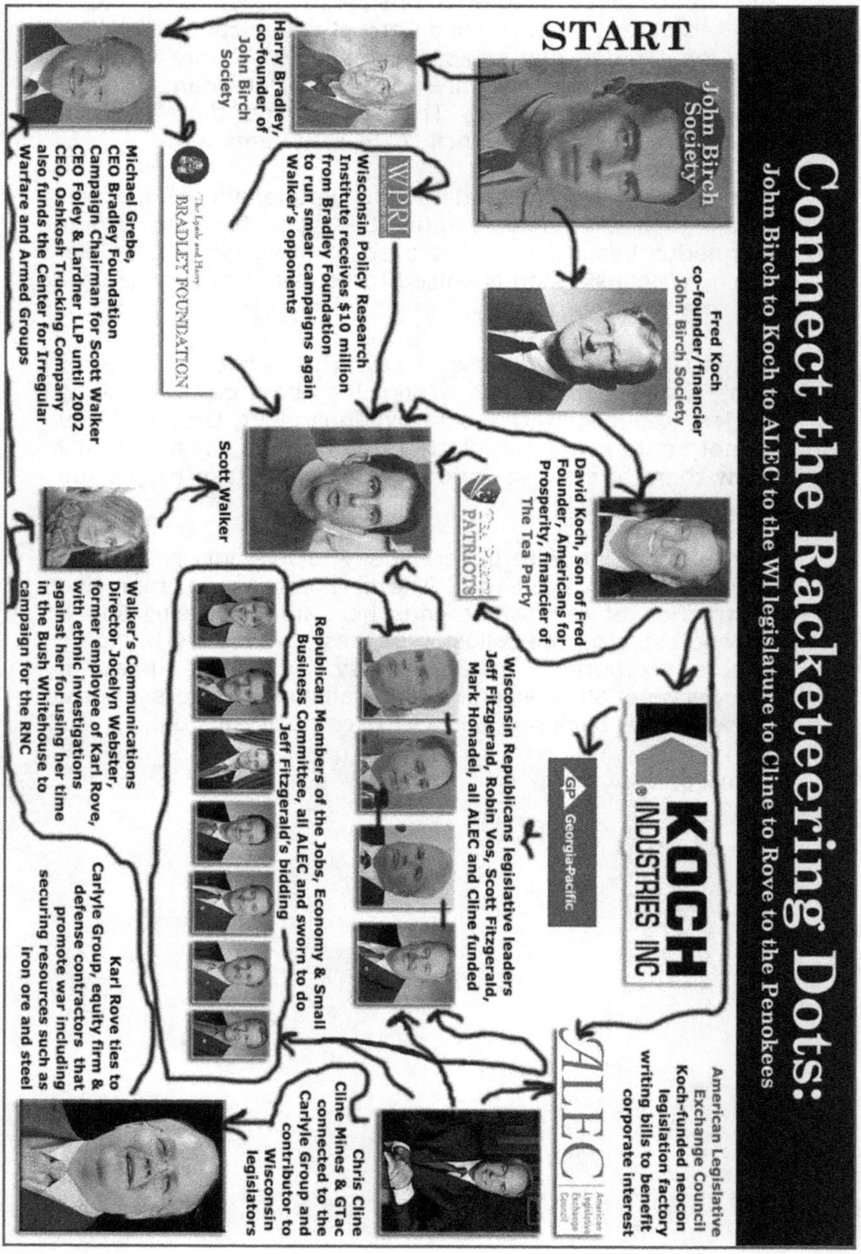
Connect the Racketeering Dots:
John Birch to Koch to ALEC to the WI legislature to Cline to Rove to the Penokees
START
John Birch Society
Fred Koch co-founder/financier John Birch Society
David Koch, son of Fred Founder, Americans for Prosperity, financier of The Tea Party
KOCH INDUSTRIES INC
Georgia-Pacific
American Legislative Exchange Council Koch-funded neocon legislation factory writing bills to benefit corporate interest
ALEC American Legislative Exchange Council
Harry Bradley, co-founder of John Birch Society
WPRI
Wisconsin Policy Research Institute receives $10 million from Bradley Foundation to run smear campaigns again Walker's opponents
The Lynde and Harry BRADLEY FOUNDATION
PATRIOTS
Scott Walker
Wisconsin Republicans legislative leaders Jeff Fitzgerald, Robin Vos, Scott Fitzgerald, Mark Honadel, all ALEC and Cline funded
Republican Members of the Jobs, Economy & Small Business Committee, all ALEC and sworn to do Jeff Fitzgerald's bidding
Chris Cline Cline Mines & GTac connected to the Carlyle Group and contributor to Wisconsin legislators
Michael Grebe, CEO Bradley Foundation Campaign Chairman for Scott Walker CEO Foley & Lardner LLP until 2002 CEO, Oshkosh Trucking Company also funds the Center for Irregular Warfare and Armed Groups
Walker's Communications Director Jocelyn Webster, former employee of Karl Rove, with ethnic investigations against her for using her time in the Bush Whitehouse to campaign for the RNC
Karl Rove ties to Carlyle Group, equity firm & defense contractors that promote war including securing resources such as iron ore and steel

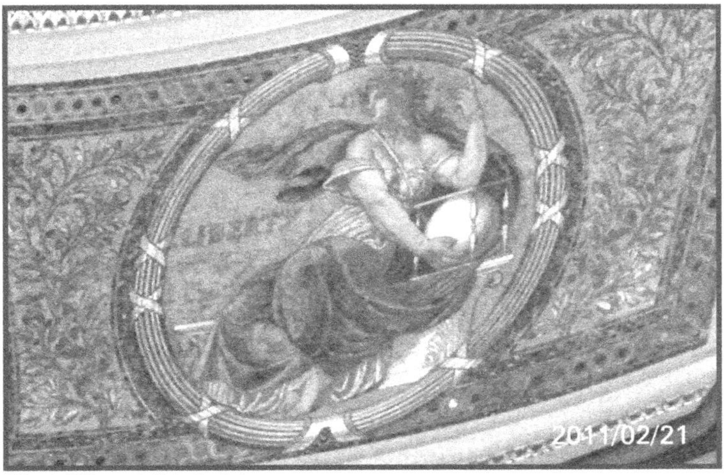

"Liberty," Wisconsin State Capitol

HISTORY OF THE TAKEOVER

If you are reading this book, chances are you or someone close to you is tremendously concerned about what's happening in the US government. If you're like me, you've watched for years as the country has systematically appeared to turn right-wing Republican. Over the past decade as more and more neoconservative candidates have taken office, maybe like me, you're wondering what's gotten into Americans that they are moving so far to the right and spewing so much hate.

On February 9, 2009, a reporter for CNBC named Rick Sanitelli delivered a scathing rant from the floor of the Chicago Mercantile Exchange.[2] Formerly a vice president for an institutional trading and hedge fund account, Sanitelli claimed his rant wasn't scripted; instead, he said he was fed up with the banking bailout and other nefarious acts taking place in Washington.

Some believe his performance, however, was merely an exuberant pitch on behalf of an elaborate network of aligned corporate interests that included the Koch brothers, billionaire owners of the largest private corporation in

2 http://www.cnbc.com/id/29283701/Rick_Santelli_s_Shout_Heard_Round_the_World

America, and scores of well-funded, right-wing think tanks and advocacy groups. Their *raison d'être*? By all appearances it was another step in the overthrow the government of the United States to install a corporate oligarchy.

Sanitelli's rant was pointedly meant to appeal to the masses of Americans who by this time were exasperated with the US "economic crisis." Out of this moment, the Tea Party was born, springing forth fully formed and subsequently mainlined by the corporate-controlled media.

Although Sanitelli's rant may have been a benchmark, it was by no means the first event designed to control the masses of disgruntled conservative Americans. We can look to 2000, the year the presidential election was stolen, as the date that marks the true foothold in the 50-year plan for the takeover.[3] Putting Bush in the White House would successfully demonstrate that they could indeed game the national elections. With a stacked Supreme Court in Washington DC, poorly-designed ballots in Florida, and Fox News ready to broadcast the steal, corruption was established on all levels of the playing field, and the stage was properly set. All the Supreme Court had to do was declare Bush the winner, and the deal of the decade was sealed.

In order to understand the breadth and depth of the plan, we must put the historical background and long-armed reach of the tentacles of Koch Industries into context. A New York Times article suggests the Kochs were actually descendents of Nazi sympathizers.[4] After Hitler committed suicide, their residual hate immigrated to America in the form of the John Birch Society, whose world headquarters are still located in downtown Appleton, Wisconsin.[5] The American Kochs appear intent on carrying out the philosophy of their heritage: world domination with no environmental protections, no civil rights, no Constitution, a privatized paramilitary, and slave labor, with them and the chosen few at the helm.[6]

Media Fraud

Taking control of the media was essential on election night 2000. The lead perpetrator was Fox News, the Rupert

3 http://www.opednews.com/articles/Murdoch-s-Minions-Helped-S-by-Bill-Hare-110720-71.html

4 http://unknownjournal.wordpress.com/2010/10/06/%E2%96%BC-report-the-kochs-their-nazi-past-american-oil-the-foundation-of-Republican-ideology/

5 http://www.jbs.org/

6 http://becauseican-2old2care.blogspot.com/2011/03/koch-world-domination-is-their-goal.html

Murdoch spin machine, although all major networks have become tightly controlled. Fox News first called the election for Bush in 2000.[7] In an interview in 2007, Larry King declared Fox, "The Republican Brand."[8] Comedy Central's John Stewart has frequently verified that Fox does, indeed, lie.

Bernie Sanders coined the term "propaganda echo chamber" to describe a group of media outlets who parrot each other's uncritical views of a single perspective, generally involving repetitive lying. This tactic is used to turn an unsupported allegation into what appears to be accepted fact.

In 2011, Fox commentator Bill O'Reilly and reporter Mike Tobin were caught red-handed lying about Wisconsin. Using footage from a violent protest in Sacramento, complete with palm trees, they purposefully misrepresented Wisconsin's peaceful protests as being violent and fueled by "union thugs." Wisconsin's response? Blow-up palm trees.[9]

During WWII, the propaganda minister of Hitler's Third Reich, Joseph Goebbels, was put in charge of press, radio, film, theater, music, literature, and publishing. Goebbels job was to implement Hitler's vision articulated in *Mein Kampf*, page 231 of the Manheim translation: "In this they proceeded on the sound principle that the magnitude of a lie always contains a certain factor of credibility, since the great masses of the people in the very bottom of their hearts tend to be corrupted rather than consciously and purposely evil, and that, therefore, in view of the primitive simplicity of their minds, they more easily fall victim to a big lie than to a little one, since they themselves lie in little things, but would be ashamed of lies that were too big. Such a falsehood will never enter their heads, and they will not be able to believe in the possibility of such monstrous effrontery and infamous misrepresentation in others."

Goebbel's practice of repeating the big lies has carried forward into the corporate press of today's modern corporatocracy. The Koch cartel sponsors the MacIver Institute, Wisconsin Policy Research Institute, Americans for Prosperity and Heartland Communications, to name a few of the modern day "think-tanks" dedicated to spreading misinformation that supports the cartel.

7 http://www.cbsnews.com/stories/2000/11/14/politics/main249357.shtml
8 http://en.wikipedia.org/wiki/Fox_News_Channel_controversies
9 http://twicsy.com/i/gKbez

Election Fraud

Out of Florida's 2000 "hanging chad" debacle came the legislative chess move, wherein the *Help America Vote Act* (HAVA) was passed. It not only required US polling places to use touchscreen voting machines, but that US taxpayers fund them.[10] Millions of government dollars were made available for counties around the country to purchase these new voting machines from Diebold, Sequoia and other shady corporations with deep ties to Rove and the Republican Party.[11] These right-wing organizations owned the "proprietary" software[12] and kept their programming in the machines untouchable, thereby allowing them access to manipulate the results. These corruptible machines could subtly over the course of ten years falsely show the country moving to the right by flipping small percentages of votes all across the board, over time, throughout virtually every county in America.

Along with the controllable, corruptible voting machines came an "education" arm of the takeover called the *Election Center.* Originally funded by the voting machine companies, the Center trained election officials and clerks how to support and defend the machines, offering PR courses such as, "Crisis Management for Voter Systems" and "How To Answer the Difficult Questions." As they changed the laws on local levels to protect the voting machine companies, statutes were quietly created to undermine the use of hand-count paper ballots. Under Section 5.85, Wis. Stats., it is a possible felony if an election worker hand counts ballots that have already been counted by a voting machine.

With former Enron accounting firm Arthur Andersen, re-packaged as Accenture, in charge of the voter registration rolls,[13] and a national voting system was installed that could potentially be regularly hacked to disenfranchise voters, manipulate elections and turn the country into what Karl Rove refers to as the "permanent Republican majority."[14]

Legislative Fraud: ALEC

How did the *Help America Vote Act* actually become enacted? In 2000, a neoconservative, Koch-driven organization known as the American Legislative Exchange Council

10 http://www.fec.gov/hava/law_ext.txt
11 http://www.motherjones.com/politics/2004/03/diebolds-political-machine
12 http://abcnews.go.com/Technology/story?id=2507434&page=1
13 http://www.contractormisconduct.org/index.cfm/1,73,221,html%20?ContractorID=5&ranking=68
14 http://www.washingtonpost.com/wp-dyn/content/article/2007/08/17/AR2007081701713.html

(ALEC)[15] emerged to begin writing the legislation that was showing up in one state house after another. ALEC members represent the "Republican Majority." Rep. Mark Pocan (D-78) has been an ALEC investigator for over ten years. He is there to keep an eye on what this potentially illegal and certainly unethical organization is doing: writing legislation designed to strip protection from individuals and eventually complete the takeover of the US government in favor of corporations. Republican members of every state legislature in the country have been helping craft the bills and then bringing them home to introduce as their own.

The extreme legislation we are currently dealing with in Wisconsin is aligned to the philosophies of ALEC, and most of our Republican legislators are or have been members. UW Madison professor Bill Cronon's[16] editorial blog about ALEC in March 2011 garnered him the wrath of the state Republicans,[17] and early on revealed the long-range planning of this rancorous organization.

Judicial Fraud

Judicial fraud is another key element to the takeover. From the stacking of the US Supreme Court by 2000 with right-wing tools for Rove to David Prosser being waved back to the bench even after the recount uncovered over 800 anomalies that rightfully should have invalidated thousands of votes, it is apparent that Americans cannot count on the third branch of the government to provide the checks and balances for which it was created. In March 2011, Dane Court Judge Sumi found Wisconsin Republicans guilty of not only breaking the Open Meetings Law but also violating the public trust, and the fascists were slowed.[18] Without Prosser back on the bench, the Supreme Court would have been tied when the challenge came before them. Prosser returned just in time to over-rule the lower court and propel this takeover forward again. Today we also know that during that trial, Justice Gableman was also receiving favors from the law firm that represented the Republicans.[19]

By overturning Sumi's ruling, Prosser handed state Republicans the keys to the kingdom. Rationalizing that the legislature does not have to obey the law, the court endorsed a brazen new attitude. Legislative "Special

---

15 http://alecexposed.org/wiki/Alec_Exposed:Community_portal
16 http://scholarcitizen.williamcronon.net/2011/03/15/alec/
17 http://www.nytimes.com/2011/03/28/opinion/28mon3.html?_r=1
18 http://www.nytimes.com/2011/05/27/us/27wisconsin.html
19 http://wcmcoop.com/members/attack-on-flanagan-exposes-profound-rightwing-hypocrisy/

Sessions" became the norm, wherein an unprecedented number of bills were rushed through committees, which were all Republican controlled. They were then sent on to the Republican-controlled Assembly to be rubber-stamped, and then over to the Senate Republican majority to do the same. There was no input allowed by Democrats in writing the bills, nor did public input affect the process or legislation. For the most part, the Majority allowed no amendments, no compromise, and with no apparent intention other than to grab as much power and as many resources as they were capable of stealing, Wisconsin citizens and Her Constitution be damned.

2008 and Obama

So what happened in 2008 with the presidential elections? If the Republicans control the voting systems, as they proved again in 2004 when Ohio became the new Florida, why did they "allow" Obama to win that year? Election fraud, after all, surely is not just Republican. In their book, *Votescam*, published in 1992, Jim Collier and his brother Ken unwittingly uncovered corruption in all levels and in both parties of the government.

According to an online Facebook post in August 2011 from Jonathan Simon of Election Defense Alliance, because of the financial crash in September 2008, including Lehman Brothers going belly up, it became impossible for the average American to believe the Cain-Palin ticket could override Obama's "hope" surge. He also speculates that Obama's election might very well have been a landslide had they not stolen at least some of the votes.

The Tea Party

Learning from their mistake, the Kochs figured they needed masses of people to flock to their rallies who would give their "astro-turfing"—their corporate-funded advocacy made to appear grassroots—a tinge of legitimacy. Not that the Kochs even needed their votes; those they could manufacture. What they needed was a cast of people to play the part of an angry mob who would represent the votes they could steal in the 2010 congressional and governors' races, and eventually the presidential race of 2012. That way, if another Lehman Brothers happened on the way to the polls, the steal would still be believable.

After Rick Sanitelli's 2009 "spontaneous" rant, the stage was set. Posing as a "grassroots" organization, in the beginning the Tea Party claimed to have no real corporate sponsor, thereby lying right out of the gate.[20] Their lies, however, attracted hundreds of thousands of well-meaning Americans with promises of fiscal conservatism and libertarian ideals. Believing the lies, masses of unfortunate people unwittingly took part in one of the farthest-reaching bamboozles of modern US history.

Fortunately, their true colors were soon publicly revealed when Australian Taki Oldham blew their cover with his documentary, *The Billionaires' Tea Party*. In it, he traveled with the party and discovered that behind the movement's rhetoric was a highly coordinated network of shadow groups, including Club for Growth, which, according to Oldham's report, were funding and fueling all levels of the hostile takeover of the government.

Bringing Together Hate

Taking a page from the family playbook, the Kochs also served to connect a network of hate groups[21] into one organized focus, fueling them with money and lies, and setting them about to cause dissension between all parties on local stages. Fox gave Glenn Beck full control to rile up the hateful masses. Even though the Tea Party appeared to pit itself against the Republican Party, in truth, it was just a giant chess game to keep the peasants fighting amongst themselves, a predictable tactic to divide and conquer.

With each crisis after 2000, the country became more and more "at risk" from alleged "outside terrorists." 9/11 cemented the Patriot Act, and Homeland Security began the police state in earnest. The shifted manipulation to the right allowed the "elected" officials to slowly eliminate personal and civil rights as a way to "protect" us.[22] Homeland Security was, after all, for our own good. We could not risk allowing foreigners into the country, for fear they may try to overthrow the government and commit acts of terror.

Little did the American public know when the Twin Towers came crashing down exactly the sort of closed society that would rise up from the ashes. This decade has been the crowning moment in the US corporate industrial war machine's quest to finally gain total control. Or so they thought.

---

20 http://www.npr.org/templates/story/story.php?storyId= 129926390

21 http://www.huffingtonpost.com/2010/12/30/tea-party-nation-naacp-hate-group_n_802651.html

22 http://www.govexec.com/defense/2004/08/lawmakers-worry-that-home-land-security-overshadows-civil-rights/17391/

We Have Met The Enemy

There are no "outside terrorists" more frightening than corporations and "elected" officials who steal our votes to install their political tools who then use their stolen power to wage war against US citizens. Add to this an apathetic citizenry that sits back and does nothing, and we have indeed met the enemy and it is us. In reality, the industrial war machine has been creating crises to use as an excuse to close our society, strip us of our rights, and turn our Democracy into a corporate oligarchy.

After a ten-year set-up and with Tea Party support reaching its zenith, the stealing of the 2010 gubernatorial and senate races of the Great Lakes states, Florida and Arizona signaled that the oligarchy had finally arrived. It appears that the corporate controllers planned for 2011 to be the year to move quickly, for they knew Americans would begin to figure it out. With the media fraudulently churning out the propaganda, they relied on the apathy of the American "sheeple" not to catch on fast enough. As people cared more how many times Lindsey Lohan went to treatment, Governor Rick Synder was quickly declaring financial martial law in Michigan. Wisconsin was to be not far behind. Had it not been for the 14 Democrats leaving the state, Wisconsin very well could have followed the way of Michigan.

Shock and Awe, And Post-Traumatic Stress

Understandably it's difficult to wrap one's mind around the idea that this type of political evil has re-emerged on Main Street, Wisconsin, but the sooner we face it, the more power we can add to the movement for reform, and the sooner we can act. The term *shock and awe* could not be more accurate for a process that leaves people incapacitated as they discover how far-reaching the corruption really is.

Shock and Awe

In 1996, Harlan K. Ullman and James P. Wade coined the term *shock and awe* to define a military strategy intended to create rapid domination over enemies. This fast-moving and hard-hitting strike is meant to "impose ... an overwhelming level of *Shock and Awe* against an adversary on an immediate or sufficiently timely basis to paralyze its will to carry on ... [to] seize control of the environment and paralyze or so overload an adversary's perceptions and understanding of events that the enemy would be incapable of resistance at the tactical and strategic levels."[23]

---

23 Harlan K. Ullman and James P. Wade, Shock And Awe: Achieving Rapid Dominance (National Defense University, 1996), XXV.

In the long-range plan of the takeover of our government, the 2010 elections can be perceived as the set-up for the Tea Party Republicans to steal the votes and once and for all embed fascism into power. Was their directive to use shock and awe, working as fast as they could without concern about re-election? Is that why everything suddenly has to be "streamlined?"

We're being hit on every level—local, state, national and international—and every issue—collective bargaining, freedom of speech, economic, educational, human and environment rights—leaving us exhausted and incapable of resistance. Is that why in 2011 almost every state in the union as well as our federal government appeared to suddenly turn militantly unreasonable?

That We the People allowed this to happen is certainly our responsibility—for not paying attention or participating in our own government. At the same time, the media ran a very tight ship in aiding and abetting in the takeover by encouraging television watching and consumptive addiction, and repeatedly broadcasting lies in the echo chamber. According to the *New York Times*, Americans average 34 hour of television a week[24]—2.5 months per year. How many hours of that is the echo chamber propaganda?

We have been trained to expect election fraud, as we slipped back into denial of a truth too distasteful to admit. In 2004, with Ohio as the new Florida, I believe We the People went numb watching our country being stolen again, right before our eyes. That night in 2004 when I went to bed with Kerry and woke up with Bush—I had to go numb. The implication was staggering and I felt so helpless in the face of this shock and awe. *Dancing With The Stars* became anesthesia for the masses. What else could we do?

Perhaps this is why most Election Integrity activists in this country suffer from post-traumatic stress. Once you see your country being stolen with your own two eyes and look directly into the face of the real terrorists who have taken control, you can never really rest again. Suddenly, the lies the media are broadcasting become not only apparent but also woefully wrong and purposefully destructive. Every person who says, "I'm just not political, sorry," as their reason not to take action seems like a traitor, too.

---

24 http://www.nytimes.com/2011/01/03/business/media/03ratings.html?_r=3&ref=media

For me, the rage I felt seeing the evidence of fraud from the Wisconsin Supreme Court recount being ignored made me want to shout the truth, louder and stronger than any of their propaganda. I knew that sooner or later, any structure built on a system for the good of the few at the expense of the whole would collapse in on itself. It's why the Kochs lost the first time around in 1945,[25] because governments all around the world took action and stood up against the Third Reich.

This time around, We the People in every country of the world have to stand up, one person at a time, for each other and the earth. We must exercise the very rights they are trying to claim aren't ours. As each individual finds and uses his or her voice, more power is added to the rising wave of change for the good of all.

I am now an official member of the Election Integrity movement. I earned my stripes driving circles around the Capitol building in Madison in a rage until 1 AM the night of August 8, 2011, the first of the Wisconsin recall elections. I underestimated the disgust I would feel on hearing that Kathy Nickolaus was again delaying the results in the district we predicted they would tamper with—Alberta Darling's seat in Senate District 8.[26]

Yes, I understand this election integrity PTSD now. As long as current voting systems are allowed to remain in place, the United States should consider itself under terrorist attack from within. I cannot rest until we ensure open, transparent and hand-counted, paper ballots elections.

Decades of Evidence

Through the years, election integrity activists have documented the evidence of election fraud around the country. From Bev Harris' meticulous research available on blackboxvoting.org;[27] to the testimony from Clifford Curtis, a programmer as to how the machines are hacked; to Princeton University's study on how easy the machines are to manipulate;[28] it's not for lack of evidence that we can't get reform. Instead we lack laws that protect the people,

25 http://unknownjournal.wordpress.com/2010/10/06/%E2%96%BC-report-the-kochs-their-nazi-past-american-oil-the-foundation-of-Republican-ideology/

26 http://bdgrDemocracy.wordpress.com/2011/08/10/recall-perspectives-bigger-than-kathy-nickolaus-and-alberta-darling/

27 http://blackboxvoting.org/

28 http://www.youtube.com/watch?v=GamR4y_ykA0

Wisconsin Constitution Article XIII, SECTION 12. Recall of elective officers.

The qualified electors of the state of any congressional, judicial or legislative district or of a county may petition for the recall of any incumbent elective officer after the first year of the term for which the incumbent was elected, by filing a petition with the filing officer with whom the nomination petition to the office in the primary is filed, demanding the recall of the incumbent.
(1) The recall petition shall be signed by electors equalling at least twenty-five percent of the vote cast for the office of governor at the last preceding election, in the state, county or district which the incumbent represents.
(2) The filing officer with whom the recall petition is filed shall call a recall election for the Tuesday of the 6th week after the date of filing the petition or, if that Tuesday is a legal holiday, on the first day after that Tuesday which is not a legal holiday.
(3) The incumbent shall continue to perform the duties of the office until the recall election results are officially declared.
(4) Unless the incumbent declines within l0 days after the filing of the petition, the incumbent shall without filing be deemed to have filed for the recall election. Other candidates may file for the office in the manner provided by law for special elections. For the purpose of conducting elections under this section:

(a) When more than 2 persons compete for a nonpartisan office,a recall primary shall be held. The 2 persons receiving the highest number of votes in the recall primary shall be the 2 candidates in the recall election, except that if any candidate receives a majority of the total number of votes cast in the recall primary, that candidate shall assume the office for the remainder of the term and a recall election shall not be held.

(b) For any partisan office, a recall primary shall be held for each political party which is by law entitled to a separate ballot and from which more than one candidate competes for the party's nomination in the recall election. The person receiving the highest number of votes in the recall primary for each political party shall be that party's candidate in the recall election. Independent candidates and candidates representing political parties not entitled by law to a separate ballot shall be shown on the ballot for the recall election only.

(c) When a recall primary is required, the date specified under sub. (2) shall be the date of the recall primary and the recall election shall be held on the Tuesday of the 4th week after the recall primary or, if that Tuesday is a legal holiday, on the first day after that Tuesday which is not a legal holiday.

(5) The person who receives the highest number of votes in the recall election shall be elected for the remainder of the term.
(6) After one such petition and recall election, no further recall petition shall be filed against the same officer during the term for which he was elected. (7) This section shall be self-executing and mandatory. Laws may beenacted to facilitate its operation but no law shall be enacted to hamper, restrict or impair the right of recall.

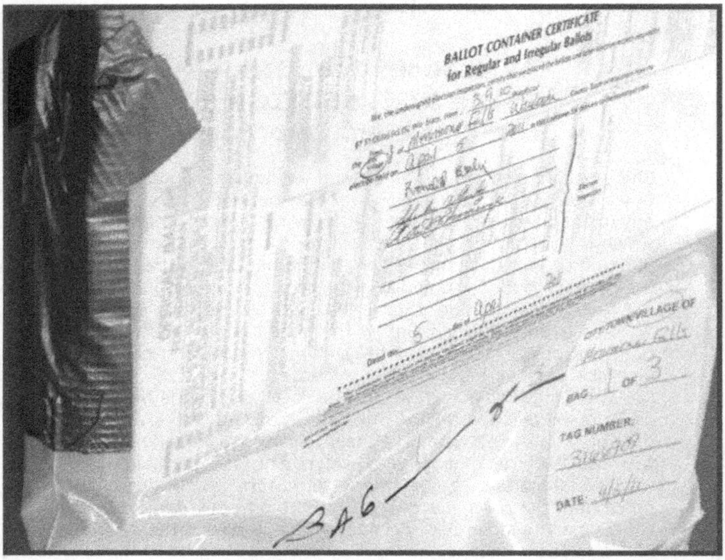

A ballot bag found in Waukesha from Menomonie Falls that had been duct taped shut. Observers asked the ballots be removed to examine the inside of the bag, as some were speculating that the bag had torn and merely needed to be taped up. On further investigation, observers stated that it appeared that the sides had been slit.

our rights and our votes. We have a corporate media that won't tell the truth, an apathetic and insensible public, and judicial and election systems in synch—a coordinated corruption—that have kept Election Integrity activists from moving this forward. It's certainly not for lack of evidence but instead lack of justice.

In this war that the Republican Tea Party launched on the country in 2011, I believe Wisconsin was given a golden ticket. When our Democrats left the state in February to allow us time to really read the budget bill, we did, and we understood their message to us. Then the Supreme Court recount gave us a glimpse into our corrupted election system, and the fifteen recall elections provided a platform to potentially install the first wave of reform.

Rising out of our shock and awe, a mighty force came to life on the ground. The people of Wisconsin organized on every level to stand strong to protect our rights. In short order, we organized the first six recall elections that summer and won two new seats in the Senate, and successfully defended against three recalls launched against the Democrats. We gathered more than enough signatures from November 2011 to January 2012 to recall the governor, Lt. Governor and four Republican Tea Party candidates. Good people have stepped up to run for office and more are coming to serve.

Stealing The Recall

On June 5, 2012 I believe, once again, the corporate-controlled election system was rigged for Walker. Not just that Walker had ten times the corporate money than his opponent,[29] Tom Barrett, but the year before, Command Central voting machine vendors started handed out, free of charge, two corruptible touchscreen voting machines for every one optech scanner, the kind that require paper ballots. Along with what we uncovered at the recount, and the blatant legislation of voter suppression the Republicans pushed through, everything about this election smelled like a steal.

According to polls, Walker and challenger Barrett were tied up until Election Day. There were record turnouts at the polls all over the state, especially in the inner city of Milwaukee that was running heavily for Barrett.[30] Yet at 8:45 PM, when votes were still being cast and counted, CNN declared Walker the winner with only 21% of the state reporting. Barrett conceded while people were still in line at the polls. As I watched the corporate media happily report another Republican victory, I knew there would be no way to know the truth, not with the way the machines can be hacked.

What I do know is that there were so many overwhelming signs that the state was ready to dump Walker. The recall that began in November showed the state just how serious we were about rejecting this corporate takeover. After two months of relentless circulation in every corner of the state through the heart of the Wisconsin winter, almost 2,000,000 signatures were collected for six recalls,[31] including Lt. Governor Kleefisch and one of the biggest ringleaders of the Republican takeover, Scott Fitzgerald. Whether you supported it or not, this display showed just how many Wisconsin citizens were intent on getting these traitors out of our government.

---

29 http://www.jsonline.com/news/statepolitics/walker-barrett-to-release-fundraising-totals-later-tuesday-gu5jgr9-155466225.html

30 http://nbcpolitics.msnbc.msn.com/_news/2012/06/05/12073979-video-big-turnout-for-wisconsin-recall-election?lite

31 http://wcmcoop.com/members/recall-petitions-turned-in-at-3-pm-now-we-must-protect-our-elections/

A recent John Doe investigation has resulted in numerous arrests of Walker associates, launched to consider alleged criminal acts of campaigning on public time and dime while he was County Executive of Milwaukee. The public has now seen the proof of the corruption in court documents showing Walker's name attached to the e-mails. Former associate Tim Russell was also charged with embezzlement[32] and Russell's partner Brian Pierick was charged with child enticement,[33] as the FBI uncovered text messages to underage boys.

Never before in US history was a state as ready, willing and able to utilize the power of recall as rigorously as Wisconsin. Our Constitution not only allows it but also protects and encourages the use of recall when citizens feel their government and Democracy are being threatened. Crimes have been committed. Democratic process and laws were ignored. The recall of Scott Walker and the other fascists was our duty and done *for all the right reasons*. If we do not find a way to rid our state of fascism, Walker and his cronies will continue to drive us into poverty, stealing our resources and destroying the fabric of our state using a billion-dollar propaganda echo chamber telling people "It's Working."[34] When our politicians refuse to protect our schools, public funds, workers, water, and air from their corporate sponsors, the state will, in fact, be destroyed if we don't stand up.

After seeing our votes stolen at last summer's recount, the whistle-blowers in Wisconsin mobilized hundreds of volunteers to protect the summer recall elections, forced the issue of election integrity at legislative committee and GAB meetings, reached out to educate county clerks and work together with legislators and election workers for reform. Because of these efforts, more and more people are being educated on the truth and how to stand up and take action. We are committed to one day longer, one day stronger, and the corporations will never wear us down. Each day that passes gives us more time to expand our efforts and widen the circle of those committed to nonviolently standing up to protect Democracy.

After Walker's steal, more and more people are willing to listen to the evidence. This in turn has breathed new life into the national Election Integrity movement, whose time

32 http://wcmcoop.com/members/scott-walkers-2-daddies-2/
33 http://www.postcrescent.com/article/20120123/APC010401/120123072/Former-Scott-Walker-associate-Tim-Russell-will-stand-trial
34 http://wcmcoop.com/members/maciver-institute-and-afp-working-for-walker-campaign/

has now arrived. Never before has the nation been ready to hear the truth and take action. Wisconsin has been given the task to start the process rolling for each and every state to follow suit until we reform elections systems throughout the nation.

The Truth Is Setting Us Free

In May 2011, a Tea Party rally in South Carolina drew about 30 people.[35] One held in La Crosse, Wisconsin netted about the same on August 5.[36] Efforts to recall Sen. Bob Jauch (D-Poplar) on the part of the Tea Party failed miserably. This undeniable decline of Tea Party support comes from the fact that average Americans are now aware of the awful truth of the Kochs, and are personally experiencing their end goal: the complete dismantling of the US government and the privatization of the country's common wealth to profit corporations.

More and more citizens understand that the passage of Citizens United,[37] which declared that corporations are "people," opened the door to unlimited and secret campaign contributions just in time for the 2010 gubernatorial and senate steals resulting in the immediate and rapid power grab on both local and national levels. This attack on US soil also includes international mining companies and their assault all across the US via their ownership of mineral rights beneath our land. Combine the removal of protection for the land, people, air, and water with the mining companies' track record of leaving behind toxic pollution, and you have environmental warfare more effective than bombs.

Make no mistake: this stand is about rights. Our message is clear: A politician who makes an oath to protect the Constitution becomes a traitor when he or she uses electively-endowed power to pass laws that strip us of our rights in the name of economic hardship on the part of the government. Politicians who choose to do that should be aware that, one way or another, they will be removed from office through sweeping grassroots reform, highly organized and designed to protect We the People. When we restore justice and take back our Democracy, corrupt politicians will be held accountable. Let's begin with election reform.

---

35 http://maddowblog.msnbc.msn.com/_news/2011/05/20/6684032-more-of-a-tea-gathering-than-a-party
36 http://www.politiscoop.com/component/content/article/35-last-24h-news/470-obituary-tea-party-rise-and-fall-rip.html
37 http://www.salon.com/2012/01/21/the_hard_truth_of_citizens_united/

Below, another of the many ballot bags found in Waukesha during the May 2011 recount of the Supreme Court election. The bag was sealed in a way that leaves plenty of room to remove and re-insert ballots.

While observing the City of Milwaukee, all materials from each ward were processed together by the same poll workers. We all sat together at tables, two poll workers and two observers. I could observe every step and see all the evidence first hand: envelopes, poll books, matched seals, matched absentees, matched envelopes, etc. Everything I saw matched, the recount ran smoothly, disputes were small, and the poll workers and observers solved the problems together. For the most part, workers all followed one basic process.

On arrival at Waukesha, I found exactly the opposite: All elements of the ward were pulled apart; some people had the poll books; others had the ballots. There were blue lines on the floor you couldn't cross if you didn't have the right tags, and there were yellow barricades between the observers and poll workers, making it harder for observers to see. Only the head clerks were allowed to put all the elements of the ward together. No one table of poll workers or observers ever saw all the elements of one polling place together. When they brought bags to the tables with mismatched seals and large gaping holes big enough to put ballots through, we had to take someone's word for the fact that this gross abuse of the handling of our votes was being recorded, and whoever was responsible for this negligence for ballot safety would eventually be held accountable. But by pulling apart all the elements of the districts, they made it impossible for observers to corroborate anything from any district, as we were able to do in the city of Milwaukee.

"Government," Wisconsin State Capitol

WISCONSIN 2011

In February 2011, Scott Walker, the newly-elected Tea Party Republican governor of Wisconsin brought forth a budget bill heard round the world. Introduced on a Friday, the Republican majority *proclaimed* they would pass the 144-page draconian budget repair bill into law the following Thursday. The bill contained, among other things, a severe reduction of public employee unions' ability to negotiate contracts. Walker claimed this aspect of Wisconsin politics was costing the state millions, and if not accepted, he would be forced to make massive layoffs because, "We're broke."

Justifying his union-busting ploy, Walker told us in February 2011 that, "the path to long-term financial solvency for our state requires shared sacrifices from everyone."[38] Later in April, Walker would come before a federal Senate Oversight and Government Reform Committee, and testify under oath that reducing unions' ability to negotiate contracts had absolutely no affect on the budget.[39] But in February 2011, corporate media was blasting his lie that unions were the cause of the fact that, "We're broke." Never mind the tax breaks Walker gave to his crony corporate friends the first

38 http://badgerherald.com/news/2011/02/13/walkers_budget_propo.php
39 http://www.youtube.com/watch?v=xqhtUTyqVOY

month he was in office that were adding $117 million to the state's budget problem over the next two years.[40] According to Walker, the bottom line was, "We're broke." Busting the unions was the only way out. This was the first big lie.

As the Democratic senators read the bill they were ordered to pass in less than a week, shock and awe set in. They knew when average Wisconsin citizens read the bill, they, too, would be horrified. Losing collective bargaining rights was just the tip of the iceberg. Suddenly, teachers and public workers were the enemy. Years of building a state that benefited the good of all, erased. Decades-long coalitions between Democrats, Progressives, Republicans and public sector unions were crushed. Raided funds were drained into black box accounts. Environmental protections—gone. Public education and health care, gutted. Tax breaks for the wealthy and the corporations at the expense of the under-privileged were prioritized above all else. Privatization of public services, state-owned power plants sold for $1, unions dismantled, public education in ruins—this Republican administration designed this budget repair bill to destroy Wisconsin.

What few average citizens knew back in February was that the "budget repair bill" was the product of the American Legislative Exchange Council (ALEC). Nor was it known that this far-right, Koch Industries-funded organization also provided the same draconian budget template for the newly-elected governors of Ohio, Indiana, Florida, and Michigan—all states with significant waterfronts. These ALEC budgets were intertwined. Partnered with other ALEC legislation about to come down the pike, the plan was intricately designed to legislate corporate free rein, allowing them to "legally" to do as they please without consequence.

As it turned out, almost every Wisconsin Republican legislator has been or is a member of ALEC, including Scott Walker and both majority leaders of each house. The 2011 Republicans appeared to have played their part in the orchestrated hostile takeover of the state. By using their offices to abuse their power of majority, they were prepared to pass bills that would violate our Constitutional rights, dismantle public education, disempower workers, wage a war against women, bankrupt communities, steal and destroy natural resources, and build in tax breaks and protections for corporations.

40 http://www.postcrescent.com/article/20110201/APC0101/102010421/Wisconsin-Governor-Scott-Walker-signs-tax-cut-bill-into-law

Following this course, as counties, cities and towns were being starved for resources because of this abuse of power, Walker could claim our finances were so bad that we eventually wouldn't be able to govern ourselves. In Benton Harbor, Michigan, elected officials were stripped of their authority and an Emergency Financial Manager was appointed, costing taxpayers $150 an hour, even though Michigan was "broke" too. In one stroke of Governor Snyder's pen and the power of the Republican majority in their legislature moving as quickly as Wisconsin might have been, Michigan citizens basically lost their right to vote. Wisconsin was not to be far behind.

In that fateful week in February, the Democratic Party legislators knew Wisconsin's budget repair bill was a hostile takeover of the most corporate kind, but they were powerless to stop it. There appeared to be no brakeman on what one senator's aide called, "The Republican Crazy Train to Nowhere."

Filibuster in Illinois

The public hearing on the budget bill was scheduled for Tuesday, February 15 before the Joint Finance Committee. Co-chair Robin Vos (R-Burlington and WI State Chairman for ALEC) announced they would hear public testimony and then vote it out of committee later that day. But thousands of people waited in long lines outside the hearing room for a chance to speak about the bill.[41] An overflow room was set up, which quickly filled. Large-screen televisions were set up in the rotunda for the approximately 4,000 who were keeping a 24-hour vigil there.

At the 17th hour of public testimony, Vos decided he'd had enough.[42] "People are talking about issues we already heard before," he declared and closed the hearing. Citizens in the hallways rebelled, chanting and demanding to be heard. Democrats opened up a hearing room after Vos shut out the public and continued testimony.[43] As long as the Democrats had the hearing room open, the rest of the Capitol had to remain open as well. People slept in the rotunda and in the hallways outside the hearing room. Later the following morning, the Democrats rested their case.

At noon that day, Vos reconvened the Joint Finance Committee and easily passed the bill through with a majority

41 http://www.jsonline.com/blogs/news/116290884.html
42 http://www.jsonline.com/blogs/news/116296034.html
43 http://www.jsonline.com/blogs/news/116297884.html

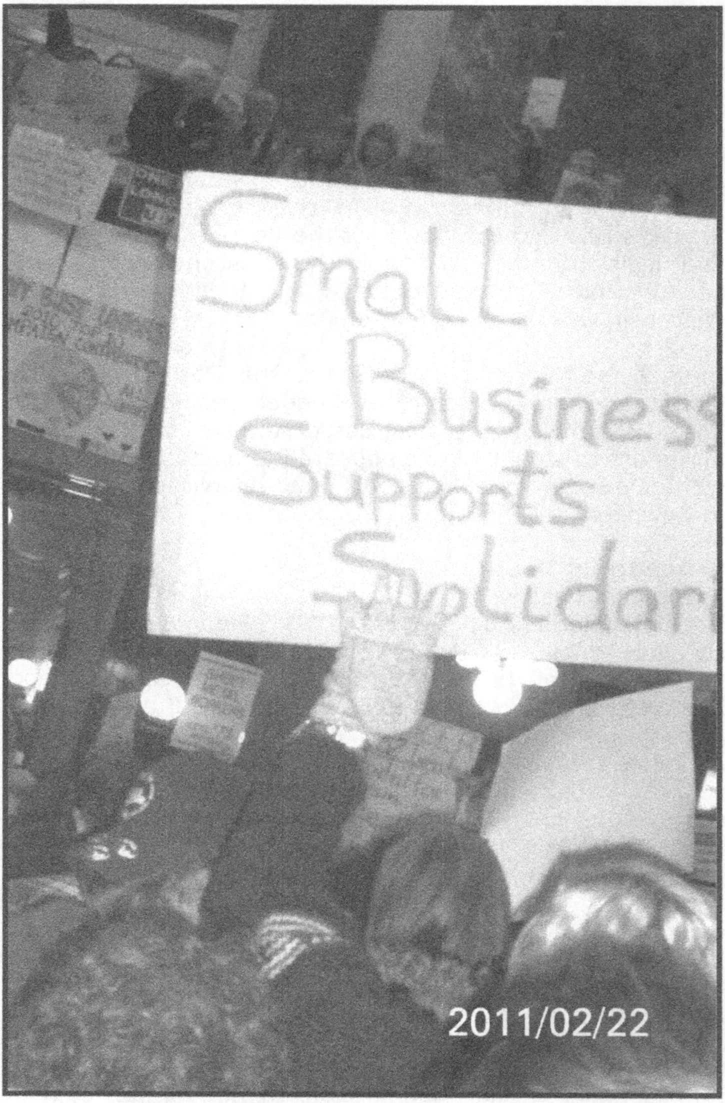

February 22, 2011, Madison Capitol. I coincidentally booked work in Madison for the second week of the month. I arrived on a Tuesday, the 14 Democratic Senators left the state the next day, and thousands flooded to the capitol to protest. For the next ten days, I became a part of and began documenting the remarkable and advantageous rise of We the People. All ages, genders, races, religions, and professions participated in weeks of demonstrations. Not just unions, all good citizens stood up all at once and, oh, what a sight it was.

party-line vote. It would have been on its way to the Senate where speaker Scott Fitzgerald (R-Juneau, member of ALEC) had a 19-14 majority. From there, it would sail on to the Assembly, where Speaker Jeff Fitzgerald (R-Horicon, member of ALEC) had a 59-39 edge. Then on to the new Governor, and Wisconsin would be in the bag.

A Little Issue of Quorum

Since the budget was a fiscal concern, a three-fifths quorum would be needed for it to pass. In the Senate, that meant at least 20 members had to be present to pass the bill, regardless of party. While Jeff Fitzgerald—Fitz the Younger—had quorum in the Assembly, Fitz the Elder needed at least one Democrat present in the Senate to call the vote.

Meanwhile, the crowds at the Capitol grew. Many camped inside overnight with more massing outside. How in the world could the 14 Democrats stop this apparent takeover of the government of Wisconsin? With Stephen "Papa" Fitzgerald the newly-appointed head of the State Patrol, and Attorney General J.B. Van Hollen a Walker supporter as well, the State of Wisconsin seemed prime pickings for the ALEC fascists. All they needed was to pass this budget, and all state resources would soon be in the hands of the corporate members of ALEC.

As they secretly met outside the Capitol building, the Democratic Senators knew they didn't have a chance against what they were up against, and that most of the state had no clue what was in the bill. With corporate media propaganda filling the airwaves about how courageous Walker was for making "tough choices," the Democrats knew the truth. This was not business as usual. This budget repair bill, brought forward pre-formed, without input from the people or the other party, would bankrupt the state. No negotiations; the Democrats were told on February 11 that they would pass a budget repair bill that neither they nor the public had any input on by February 17. Even after hours of public hearings, nothing in it changed. So now what?

Rumor has it that the night the Democratic Senators fled the state, one rogue Republican leaked the news to his friend from the other side of the aisle over cocktails: Senate Republicans were going to do a "call to the house" procedure. This procedure would basically lock them into the Senate and force the vote on the budget repair bill. Since the Republicans had the majority and only needed one Democrat present for quorum, it was "go time" for the Democratic Senators. Whatever they were to do, they all had to sign on to the plan. If even one of them stayed behind, it would be for naught.

At some point, they all agreed to leave the state. Not knowing how long they'd be gone, they grabbed overnight bags and planned to meet up at the Clock Tower Inn in Rockford, Illinois, a famous midway point between Madison and Chicago. There they would regroup and figure out the next step. They hoped that by leaving the state as a way to filibuster this unfathomable budget repair bill, the rest of us would have a chance to learn what they knew. But what to do once they arrived in Rockford? And how would citizens respond to their leaving? These were two entirely unexplored questions in Wisconsin politics.

When The Cat's Away

With the Democrats gone, Walker launched his assault not only on public workers of the state, but on the Democratic Senators and their staff. The Senate Republicans, using the power of their newly-acquired majority, passed a ludicrous series of resolutions to discredit the Democrats. Their staff was ordered to report to Republican Senators; they were charged $100 a day for their absence; they now had to pick up their paychecks on the Senate floor instead of direct deposit. Senate Republicans voted to send the State Patrol officers to their homes to arrest them, an action whose legality was easily questioned. But perhaps the most ridiculous was the resolution to dismantle their copier codes and cut off access to copy machines.[44]

From the start, Republican hubris has been their Achilles' heel. Walker and his lackeys lied about their intentions from the start.[45] They would eventually ignore restraining orders, pass bills in secret, steal resources, create rules to limit freedom of speech, the right to assemble and to petition the government, and begin arresting citizens for no reason at all. At every turn, they would lie outright, with the corporate media getting their backs. In all, they stopped working for us as public servants. Abandoning their oath to protect the Wisconsin Constitution, they pledged their allegiance to corporations, demonstrated by openly locking us out of the

---

44 http://www.huffingtonpost.com/2011/03/02/wisconsin-gop-senators-absent-Democrat-staff_n_830414.html

45 http://www.theawl.com/2011/03/a-blueprint-for-a-takeover-wisconsin-Republicans-lied-while-the-kochs-schemed

process and passing ALEC-authored bills that stripped away our rights, and left our land, air and water vulnerable and open to the highest bidder.

Even though the Democrats' sojourn to Illinois was not illegal, the propaganda machines churned into full spin. Painting the Democrats as cowards, right-wing talk-radio stations frothed up the loyal masses, keeping them blind to the truth of the hostile takeover. Certainly, without knowing the rest of the story, the protesters look scary, especially with Fox News falsely advertising a violent protest from Sacramento as having taken place in Wisconsin.[46] The rest of the country was being told that the people occupying the Capitol round the clock were violent union thugs, paid out-of-state agitators, hippies, dirty slobs and every other name in the book to distract from the real issues: the tyranical rule stealing our Democracy, and the awful consequences of the bill.

In truth, the peaceful protests were filled with citizens from every walk of life and every corner of Wisconsin—teachers, geologists, small business owners, students, cops, consultants, fire fighters, private sector workers of all kinds, farmers. Officially begun on February 14, when the UW Teaching Assistants' Association delivered valentines to Governor Walker, begging him to have a heart and not dessimate Wisconsin's outstanding public education system, no one paid anyone to it. Trust me, we did not need any "out-of-state agitators." We the people were riled about the stealing of our Democracy by the targeting public workers, especially teachers. We became fiercely protective of the people in whose hands we put our children. Most protesters were acting from an innate sense of protecting the children, civic duty, a long history of political engagement and a deep love of Wisconsin.

Back in February 2011, knowing the Democrats were out there somewhere, with the Capitol occupied 24/7, the whole world was watching as we all waited for the other shoe to drop.

We the People of The Great State of Wisconsin

Unbeknownst to us all, something miraculous began to take shape. With the Democrats looking on helplessly from Illinois as the Republicans broke law after law, the citizens of the

46 http://www.youtube.com/watch?v=aOzerRfB27o

state of Wisconsin stood up all at once. Trained through years of successful coalition building, bred to serve community and family, highly educated with a rich tradition of peace and justice woven into the fabric of our culture, Wisconsin stood up—a mighty waking force—and together we set up shop to protect our state. Like Donald Driver grabbing an Aaron Rodgers' Hail Mary, We the People of Wisconsin took the ball and ran like the wind.

Without knowing what we were doing, Wisconsin's true nature took over. Intuitively, people started taking action—to protest, to file law suits, to testify, to make phone calls, to do nonviolence training, to recount, to drum, to organize recalls, to write editorials, to educate our neighbors, to livestream events at the Capitol—to do everything we could to protect Wisconsin from the takeover. In every bar and coffee shop across the state, people were becoming educated, engaged and aware of what was happening around them.

February 17, 2011 Madison, Wisconsin Capitol rotunda. Photo: Rebecca Kimble

Before this, I had paid little attention to politics, but now I couldn't sit down. I discovered WisEye.com, the service that broadcasts and records all legislative sessions. I listened nonstop to sessions and committee meetings. Glued to my computer day and night when I was not in Madison, I tuned into the videos that were streaming from the Capitol daily.

What I saw was that Wisconsin took a mighty shake and called upon the power of our roots, our vision and our deep love for the Earth to begin a movement that was desperately needed and long overdue: to wake the hell up.

As the weeks wore on, hundreds of thousands of people descended on the Capitol in a show of support for our rights. The Madison police came out early to stand with Democracy, even though their union would allegedly be exempt from the bust (which later proved to be another lie). They made the choice not to become "palace guards" for Walker's takeover. They'd work their shifts, and then many went home to change and came right back to protest as private citizens. The day before Walker illegally closed the Capitol, the police slept over with the rest of the people.

This Is A Peaceful Protest
For me, a peace activist who has traveled the world teaching a new process of nonviolence, this display from my home state was breath-taking. Everyone who showed up was committed to being nonviolent. *This is a peaceful protest* was our mantra. Those words were posted on the backs of signs, a constant reminder as we marched. If someone escalated, the people in the crowd kindly reminded them of their commitment to peace, which instantly defused them. The crowd became self-monitoring, but in truth, there wasn't much to monitor. More of a community celebration, one of the most beneficial parts about the protests was making new friends, connecting grassroots together and drawing empowerment to continue our stand for our rights.

I asked around, "Who told everyone to do this?" Seems our long-established peace and justice network kicked into gear early on and trained the protestors to commit to nonviolence. It worked.

Throughout the long weeks of gathering crowds at the Capitol that winter, there was little if any crime. Not one incident of theft was reported from the hundreds of thousands of people who moved in and around the Capitol. Try as the Republicans would to spin this as violent, it remained peaceful, and was having just the opposite effect—neighbors from all around the state were meeting in the protest lines, joining forces, making friends and becoming part of a movement that once it got flowing, simply could not be contained.

The citizens of Wisconsin have worked long and hard, for generations, to make this a state worth living in. Peace and justice are woven into the fabric of who we are. Our heritage is to stand up for the little guy and protect the disenfranchised. Our forefathers have faithfully and reverently understood their obligation to be stewards of the earth. We instinctively knew to pull together to protect our rights. Thinking of how Wisconsin responded when the Democrats left still brings tears to my eyes.

March 9, 2011
On March 9, 2011, Wisconsin Republicans, led by Sen. Scott Fitzgerald broke the law to proclaim that despite weeks of telling us told how broke collective bargaining was making the state, suddenly it wasn't a fiscal issue. Stripping all the budgetary items from Act 11 (Walker's Budget Repair Bill), they created Act 10, specifically designed to destroy the unions. Here is a detailed account of the first of many legislative steals the Republicans began conducting.

Remembering March 9th
Published March 9, 2012, Wisconsin Citizens Media Coop
By Michael Matheson, Brenda Konkel, Rebecca Kemble

> *Sometime around 4:00 pm on Wednesday, March 9, 2011, several State Troopers assigned to the Wisconsin State Capitol laughed and cheerily exclaimed, "Here she comes again," as Rachel Veum, the Senate's Records and Forms Management Specialist awkwardly ran past them in her wooden clogs. In her hand, Rachel held a notice of a meeting for a Joint Committee of Conference to take place at 6:00 pm that day. That notice required the signatures of Senate Majority leader Scott Fitzgerald and his brother, Assembly Speaker Jeff Fitzgerald, the presiding officers for the Joint Committee of Conference meeting, prior to being officially posted.*
>
> *Veum obtained the signature of Senator Fitzgerald minutes later on the floor of the Senate. She then proceeded to Representative Jeff Fitzgerald's office but was unable to locate him. Ultimately, while noisily hastening through the Capitol in her clogs, the assemblyman was located in the office of his brother. She proceeded to make copies of the notice and post them at three locations: the Senate bulletin board, on a board resting on an easel located at the top of the steps outside of the vestibule of the Senate Chambers, and on the Assembly bulletin board. It was well after 4:00 pm before any notices of the meeting had been posted.*
>
> *At 4:24 pm on March 9, 2011, Rachel Veum e-mailed a scanned copy of the Joint Committee of Conference meeting notice to Dick Wheeler, at his request. The*

publisher of the on-line news service, The Wheeler Report may have personally observed Veum's dash through the Capitol. Perhaps the most widely available notice of the Committee Conference was posted on the Wheeler Report shortly afterwards. Jeff Renk, a staffer with the Senate Chief Clerk's office, published the notice on the Capitol web page shortly after the days final page update at 5:00 pm. At 5:15 pm he called the technical department to make sure that the information would be updated before 6:00 pm.

Although the Supreme Court of the State of Wisconsin would later rule that the unusual antics concerning the notice of the meeting for a Joint committee of Conference on March 9, 2011 were within the Constitutional powers of the Senate's Republican leadership,[47] the meeting had been planned since at least the 7th of March. On that Monday, Bob Lang, the Director of the Legislative Fiscal Bureau, was asked to remove all of the fiscal items from Assembly Bill 11, Scott Walker's "Budget Repair Bill." This tactic removed the Constitutional requirement for a quorum in the Senate. While all 14 Senate Democrats remained in Illinois, the Republican majority had decided to vote not on fiscal items, but on removing the rights of public employees to collectively bargain.

In the days leading up to March 9, 2011 Wisconsin citizens had experienced something unusual and unprecedented in the history of the State: The doors of the Capitol had been locked.[48] Shortly after the Assembly's questionable vote on AB11 during the early morning hours of February 25,[49] the Department of Administration began implementing a series of restrictive policies, including security checkpoints, culminating with a complete lock down of the building during the last week of February.[50] That Friday, police began handing out a flier announcing that the Capitol would be cleaned beginning at 4:00 pm and restricting sleeping locations and items permitted in the building.[51] Shortly afterwards, the police union announced that their members would be sleeping over that night.[52]

47 http://www.jsonline.com/news/statepolitics/123859034.html

48 http://www.thedailypage.com/media/2011/02/28/Pocan%20statement%20on%20 Capitol%20lockdown%20022811.pdf

49 http://www.youtube.com/watch?v=uZALlaMA9b0&feature=related

50 http://www.thedailypage.com/daily/article.php?article=32538

51 http://www.jsonline.com/blogs/news/116914523.html

52 http://www.dane101.com/current/2011/02/25/wisconsin_professional_

Although initially able to maintain the occupation of the Capitol, the last protestors left,[53] by their own accord,[54] on Thursday, March 3 in response to a court order.[55]

That Thursday, University of Wisconsin Police Chief Susan Riseling reported that 41 rounds of .22-caliber ammunition had been discovered scattered around the Capitol grounds. The Madison Police Department also announced that live ammunition had been scattered throughout the City-County Building.[56] The discoveries were made at the very moment attorneys were arguing in the courtroom of Judge John Albert concerning the access policies at the Capitol. Judge Albert would rule later that afternoon that the protesters must leave when the building closes,[57] but that the DOA must "open the state Capitol to all members of the public and rescind the access policies put in place (Monday) and replace them with the access policies in effect on Jan. 28, 2011." It would be almost two months before the Walker Administration complied with this order.[58]

Restrictions to access of the Capitol spurred outrage, confusion, and absurdity. On Tuesday March 1st, Dane County Sheriff Dave Mahoney withdrew his deputies announcing they would not serve as "palace guards." Legislators found entering their work place difficult if not impossible, including Republican Sen. Glenn Grothman who provocatively strolled among a crowd of angry protestors, only to find that his access to the building was equally restricted.[59] On Wednesday March 2nd, retired Congressman Dave Obey was denied entrance to the building to attend the 100th anniversary of the Joint Finance Committee.[60] Responding to their constituents' inability to enter the Capitol, several Assembly Democrats moved their desks on to the lawn.[61]

---

police_association_calls_for_ Capitol_to_be_kept_open_annou
53 http://www.jsonline.com/news/statepolitics/117370363.html
54 http://www.youtube.com/watch?v=mGUZyN_PYXI&feature=related
55 http://www.prwatch.org/news/2011/03/10234/wisconsin-governor-defies-court-order-open- Capitol
56 http://www.cityofmadison.com/incidentReports/incidentDetail.cfm?id=11910
57 http://host.madison.com/wsj/news/local/govt-and-politics/article_e1975d48-45cd-11e0-bcc6-001cc4c03286.html
58 http://www.chicagotribune.com/news/local/breaking/chi-metal-detectors-removed-from-wisconsin- Capitol-20110622,0,2679458.story
59 http://vimeo.com/20541523
60 http://www.youtube.com/watch?v=H5SIyYzmJSU
61 http://www.youtube.com/watch?v=Zg8bN72GWwA&feature=related

On Thursday March 3, Assemblyman Nick Milroy attempted to enter the building to retrieve some clothing from his office. While asserting his rights as a Legislator, Milroy was tackled by law enforcement.[62] *In a statement Milroy said, "Law officers are doing the best they can with the orders given to them. I think they're doing a great job but because they come from every corner of the state, it's hard for a good communication system. The rules keep changing... who can keep up with the confusion."*

By Monday March 7, confusion still reigned. Public access to the Capitol remained restricted,[63] *with airport type security protocols, severely limiting the ability of people to enter.*[64] *Protest was prohibited outside of the ground floor. On Tuesday, the Capitol Police issued a list of items prohibited from the building, including vuvuzelas, crock pots, massage chairs, balloons, and trash can lids. By this time, a team of staff from the Legislative Reference Bureau and the Legislative Council offices were performing the task of removing fiscal items from Assembly Bill 11. The finished work would be in the hands of Senate Majority Leader Scott Fitzgerald the following day, Wednesday March 9, 2011.*

In the wake of a large rally the previous Saturday,[65] *the Capitol was relatively calm that Wednesday. Access was limited to two doors, the King Street and North Hamilton Street entrances. Around 3:00 pm, Deputy Capitol Police Chief Dan Blackdeer decided to release many of the on-duty officers because it "had been a very slow day." At approximately 4:00 pm, Capitol Police Chief Charles Tubbs called Blackdeer and informed him that, "Something would be happening in the Senate" that night and not to release any more people. News of the Joint Committee of Conference spread through social networks around 5:00 pm and people began flocking to the Capitol. At that very time, Senate Sergeant at Arms Ted Blazel requested officers to be sent to the Senate Chambers and Senate Parlor, where the meeting was scheduled to occur. Because of an insufficient number of officers on duty, the decision was made to close the North Hamilton Street entrance to the Capitol.*

---

62 http://www.youtube.com/watch?v=4mENJcE3Sm4&feature=related
63 http://wispolitics.com/1006/110304DOA_access.pdf
64 http://www.youtube.com/watch?v=0ExU_Xa9NgA
65 http://www.youtube.com/watch?v=wgNuSEZ8CDw

As 6:00 pm approached, the line of people attempting to enter the Capitol grew longer. Entry was stunted by the security protocol, as the crowd of over a hundred people grew increasingly apprehensive. Two young men, starting at the very end of the line, informed the waiting crowd that they were going to pull the pins on the two locked doorways on either side of the entrance. They advised people to rush into the vestibule. Moments later the doors flew open, and the crowd rushed into the building. Initially loud and raucous, chanting, "Let us in,"[66] *then using the "peace sign" to indicate quiet for communication, law enforcement agreed that everyone could enter the building after passing through screening.*

The Joint Committee of Conference Meeting was convened at 6:03 pm. In attendance were Senator Scott Fitzgerald (R-Juneau), Senator Michael Ellis (R-Neenah), Representative Jeff Fitzgerald (R-Horicon), Representative Scott Suder (R-Abbotsford) and Representative Peter Barca (D-Kenosha). Senator Scott Fitzgerald presided. Each was provided, for the first time, with a memorandum from Bob Lang containing the modifications to AB 11.

Around 6:05 pm as the crowd grew in the hallways around the Senate Parlor, Representative Barca questioned the legality of the meeting under the Open Meetings Law.[67] *While expressing his objections of the failure to give 24-hour notice and the fact that he had not received or reviewed the Lang memorandum prior to the meeting, roll was called and the Republican committee members quickly voted to recommend adoption of Conference Substitute Amendment 1 and adjourned. They then rose in unison and exited the parlor. Peter Barca remained to explain his objections to the press and the 20 people who had been admitted to the meeting. He was asked if the Senate planned to "go to the floor tonight." His response to the question was delivered barely two minutes before the Senate reconvened in special session, "That I do not know, you'll have to ask them."*

Sometime around 5:40 pm, law enforcement had escorted 24 people into the center Senate Gallery. The seats in the side galleries were empty when the Capitol

66 http://www.youtube.com/watch?v=RhO89M_fpHs&feature=youtu.be
67 http://www.youtube.com/watch?v=rUA1DJIJOZs

Police locked the doors because of the security breach at the King Street entrance to the Capitol. Outside the Senate Parlor and Chamber, it was not clear what was actually occurring.[68] Upon adjournment of the Conference Committee, many reporters had returned to the Press Room. People in the hallways, checking for information on their smart phones, exchanged conflicting accounts of the proceedings. In fact, at 6:14 pm the Senate reconvened and adopted the Joint Committee of Conference report on AB 11, Conference Substitute Amendment 1, immediately messaged it to the Assembly and adjourned at 6:22 pm.[69] Only one Senator voted against the measure, Dale Schultz (R-Richland Center).[70] Confused by the initial adjournment of the Conference Committee, reporters began scrambling into the hallway to cover the vote.

March 9, 2011. Rep.Spanbauer (R-Oshkosh) telling the press, "This lockdown of the Capitol is a stain on our democracy." Photo: Rebecca Kemble

Around this time the closing of the Capitol was announced over it's public address system, ironically noting that the closing was under the court order of Judge John Albert, the same order that had instructed the DOA to open all of the doors to the building. At some point during these events, law enforcement had locked all of the doors. The several hundred people gathered inside declined to obey the order to leave as hundreds more amassed outside of the building.[71] Over the course of the next hour and a half, the crowd inside the Capitol slowly grew in number as law enforcement directed its limited resources to contain security breaches around the building. People opened ground floor windows in bathrooms and some legislative offices. Others planned

68 http://host.madison.com/wsj/news/local/govt-and-politics/article_8747fa04-4a74-11e0-8e6b-001cc4c03286.html

69 http://www.wiseye.org/Programming/VideoArchive/EventDetail.aspx?evhdid=3880

70 http://www.youtube.com/watch?v=-S-cc9_CrTc&feature=youtu.be

71 http://www.youtube.com/watch?v=UJBbdVJ9G0U&feature=related

elaborate distractions to misdirect officers while doors were opened at opposite ends of the building. As the crowd grew, people grouped together to block lines of sight, allowing still more people into the building.

March 9, 2011. Rep. Barca confronts Capitol police chief Tubbs on why he and the people are locked out of the Assembly. Photo: Rebecca Kemble

For more than an hour the law enforcement officers assigned to the Wisconsin State Capitol attempted to maintain a security perimeter as the crowd outside grew into the thousands. By 8:00 pm, in a hopeless situation, they stood down and people streamed into the building. Shortly afterwards, Capitol Police Chief Charles Tubbs was observed in the Rotunda inquiring, "Who's in charge?"[72] For this night, the people were in charge. It is estimated that 7000 people stormed the Wisconsin State Capitol on the evening of March 9, 2011.[73]

Amidst the chaos, the 19 Republican Senators left the Capitol under heavy guard. They were secreted off on a commandeered Madison Metro Bus.[74] The crowd inside the building continued to grow as cars paraded around the inner and outer rings of the Capitol Square honking, "This is what Democracy looks like."[75]

The occupation would continue through the remainder of the night, waning in the early morning hours of March 10th, when Capitol Police were able to once again lock the building down. Some slept in the hallway blocking the office of Republican Assembly Speaker Jeff Fitzgerald, positioning themselves in a final act of civil disobedience against the passage of the bill. The Assembly was scheduled to reconvene that morning at 11:00 am. While police physically removed the demonstrators, Assembly Democrats found themselves locked out of the building.[76] Some climbed through the office windows of their colleagues, others waited. After

72 http://vimeo.com/20862247
73 http://youtu.be/TEFGKWZCA9U
74 http://youtu.be/NkaN5mjAzV4
75 http://youtu.be/YdWmP8I3i6g
76 http://youtu.be/sasa0OiKpcA

finally gaining admittance to the building, they found themselves locked out of the Assembly Chambers.

It would later be revealed that much of the delay of that morning was not due to the disruption caused by civil disobedience, but by Bob Lang, the Director of the Legislative Fiscal Bureau. He had determined that Conference Substitute Amendment 1, passed by the Joint Committee of Conference on March 9th, actually contained fiscal items. He prepared another memorandum, dated it March 10, 2011, and distributed it by e-mail at 11:50 am that morning.

Shortly after 3:30 pm, by a vote of 53-42, the Assembly passed 2011 Wisconsin Act 10.

Recall, Arrest, Repeal

Outraged at the obvious abuse of power taking place, We the People rose up to organize recalls of all possible Republican legislators who could be subject to it. Citizens all across the state took to the streets for weeks, knocking on doors, standing on street corners, collecting signatures from friends and family, all in an effort to remove the traitors who were breaking the law, stealing our votes, trampling our rights and selling our state.

By the time the first round of recalls were being organized, we as a state were beginning to see the long road ahead. No matter how fast we worked, those engaged in the takeover had now proven they would break the law to move their agenda through at lightening speed. But apparently, they underestimated the good citizens of the state and our intention to stand strong against the takeover. Recall efforts were highly organized, collecting signatures at a record pace. While we had to wait until November to start the recall of Walker, in Spring 2011, eight Republicans and four Democrats were eligible; six Republicans and three Democrats ended up being challenged.

The illegal March 9 operation to pass the bill in secret was challenged in court and Dane County Circuit Court Judge MaryAnn Sumi issued a restraining order to prevent the bill from becoming law until it could be tried. The Republicans once again flipped the entire state the bird as they declared that their illegally-passed budget bill was going to be law no matter what was legal. But when Walker ordered Secretary of State Doug La Follette to break the law himself and publish the bill, La Follette refused.

So what! The Republicans pushed right past him and declared they would enact it anyway. *How dare the judicial branch think it can rule over the legislative branch,* Scott Fitzgerald's spin went. Falling on deaf ears, yet *another* blatant criminal act only reminded us that we know full well our Republic was constructed to have checks and balances for this very reason. This was Civics 101 and yet, the corporate media persistently ran Walker and Fitzgerald's sound bytes over and over, aiding and abetting in their cause to steal government.

The case finally came before Judge Sumi and she eventually declared that Scott Fitzgerald and the Republicans did indeed violate Wisconsin Open Meetings Law.[77] In her ruling dated May 26, 2011, Sumi speaks expressly of the violation of Open Meeting Law, not ruling on Act 10 itself:

> *First, the evidence supporting the finding of violation is clear and convincing. This was not a case in which proper notice was missed by a few minutes of an hour. Not even the two-hour notice justifies "good cause" ... was provided. The legislators were understandably frustrated by the stalemate existing on March 9, but that does not justify jettisoning compliance with the Open Meetings Law in an attempt to move the Budget Repair Bill to final action.*
>
> *Second, the Legislature had the opportunity to promptly correct the violation and thus eliminate the case entirely. It could have provided timely notice of a new Committee meeting and convened the meeting in an open and public location. It has not yet done so. Even if the legislators believe that they did not violate the Open Meetings Law, convening a new meeting would not require an admission of violation and would have prevented the needless expenditure of taxpayer money to continue this lawsuit.*
>
> *Third, the rights violated by Open Meetings Law violations are public, not private. Those rights belong to all Wisconsin citizens not just those who could not gain entrance to the March 9 proceedings.*
>
> *Finally, and perhaps most significantly, the court must consider the potential damage to public trust and confidence in government if the Legislature is not held to the same rules of transparency that it has created*

77 http://www.jsonline.com/news/statepolitics/122657299.html

for other governmental bodies. Our form of government depends on citizens' trust and confidence in the process by which our election officials make laws, at all levels of government.

For all of these reasons, and under the authority vested in the circuit court, it is necessary to void the legislative action on March 9 and 10, 2011.

Conclusion: Less than one year ago our Supreme Court stated: "Open records and Open Meetings Laws, that is, 'Sunshine Laws,' are first and foremost a powerful tool for everyday people to keep track of what their government is up to ... the right of the people to monitor the people's business is one of the core principles of Democracy."

This case is exemplar of values protected by the Open Meetings Law: transparency in government, and respect for the rule of the laws. It is not this court's business to determine whether 2011 Wisconsin Act 10 is good public policy or bad public policy; this is the business of the Legislature. It is this court's responsibility, however, to apply the rule of law to the facts before it.

Later the Republican spin announced that the law did not apply to the legislators, as they had the power to override the Open Meetings Law. What the spin left out was that this was covered in the trial, too. Turned out even overriding the Open Meetings Law has rules to follow, which the Republicans did not on March 9. And as the report from WCMC reveals, this meeting was not an emergency. It was, indeed planned at least a week in advance.

Appeals were immediately filed against Judge Sumi's ruling and now the case had nowhere to go but straight to the Supreme Court.

(The Republicans however, learned from this mistake. They began to call their "Extraordinary Sessions," which allowed them to give only two-hours notice to fast track every ALEC-inspired bill they possibly could through both chambers before the session ended. Openly abusing their power of office to enact legislation that directly opposed the US Constitution, they made sure to follow the special meetings rules.)

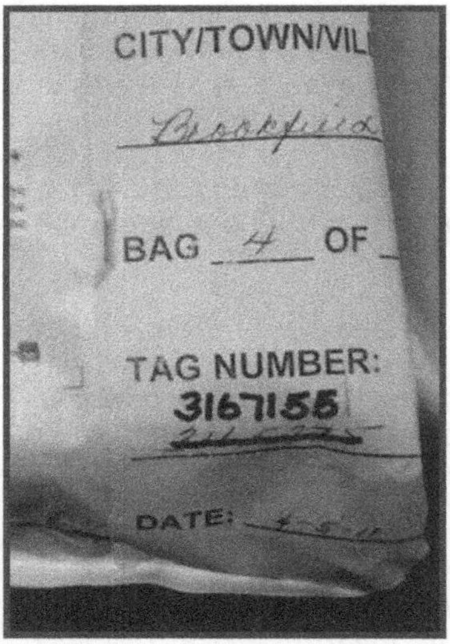

A ballot bag photographed in Waukesha during the recount, one from Brookfield, where the "missing" 14,000 ballots were discovered two days after Joanne Kloppenburg was declared the winner. Kathy Nickolaus, Waukesha County Clerk and former aide to "winner" David Prosser, was overseeing the bags in question during the recount. She was found guilty of breaking the law, but only given a slap on the wrist because she allegedly "didn't mean it."

Kloppenburg-Prosser Supreme Court Race

Coincidentally, that April was the hotly-contested race for the Supreme Court bench. Assistant Attorney General JoAnne Kloppenburg was facing off against incumbent David Prosser, a self-declared Republican with a history of anger management issues and partisan legal infractions. Prosser's former assistant Kathy Nickolaus was in charge of elections in Waukesha County. In 2001, Nickolaus was granted immunity to testify about her role as a computer analyst for the Assembly Republican Caucus, then under investigation for using state resources to secretly run campaigns. In 2002, Republican lawmakers Steven Foti, Scott Jensen and Bonnie Ladwig, as well as aide Sherry Schultz were criminally charged and later convicted in connection to using state resources to run political campaigns.[78]

With a repeated history of "human error" and faulty election results, Nickolaus was to play a pivotal role in the 2011 judicial race. Two days after the election was called for Kloppenburg, Nickolaus came forward to claim she "found" 14,000 ballots in Brookfield, which made Prosser the winner. Even with the extra votes, Prosser's lead was 7,316 votes—or 0.488%—over Kloppenburg, entitling Kloppenburg to a state-sponsored recount, since the margin was less than one-half-of-one-percent. Had Nickolaus found a few extra votes, there quite possibly would not have been a recount, and the need for election reform would never have been uncovered. Thanks to someone's bad math, the entire State had a chance to discover just how corrupt our election systems are.

78 http://host.madison.com/wsj/news/local/govt-and-politics/elections/article_6386782e-614f-11e0-97e5-001cc4c002e0.html

I was an observer at that recount. Over 800 anomalies were ignored, so many that we were literally nauseated each day watching as bag after bag of compromised ballots got counted. To this day, no one has explained the Eagle touchscreen poll tape from Pewaukee dated March 30, 2011 1:40 AM, for an election held on April 5. One feasible theory is someone went in the week before and printed up votes. After all, Prosser's place on the bench was even more urgent now that the courts were legally stopping the takeover, and Kloppenburg had a grassroots momentum. They were neck and neck. Why not plan ahead and print out some extra votes to match the machine counts and stuff the ballot bags with them for two days before declaring you found them?

Between all the observers, thousands of pictures were taken to document the evidence that cast thunderclouds of reasonable doubt that this election had been conducted in a fair and open way. Based on this evidence, Kloppenburg filed a formal complaint against Kathy Nickolaus with the GAB, but conceded to Prosser.

Nickolaus has been portrayed as an inept but well-meaning county clerk, but the magnitude of evidence of election tampering suggests that Nickolaus' previous association with political activities may not have ended with the caucus scandal. Prosser was quickly declared the winner by the GAB and waved right back to the bench, to take his place to overturn Sumi's ruling a week later.

Onward marched the takeover and now they were headed to my neck of the woods: Cline Mines and their subsidiary, Gogebic Taconite (G-Tac) was being allowed to re-write the mining laws of the state and were readying to start blowing the tops off 22 miles of the Penokee Hills on the shores of Lake Superior for an open pit iron ore mine. How could this be? It was just insane.

National Election Protection

Unbeknownst to me, while I was observing the gaming in Waukesha, sick to my stomach with nowhere to turn, Election Integrity experts from around the world had their eagle eyes on Wisconsin. One was my future friend and patriot Jeannie Dean, who calls herself a *Election Field Investigator* after spending two years filming every aspect of the notorious election in Sarasota County's FL-13 Congressional Race in which 18,412 votes "disappeared" from the county's touchscreen voting machines. She was following the live audio feed of the Wisconsin recount for weeks and was listening when I actually discovered the March 30 poll tape.

Watching for myself as the Republicans stole the Supreme Court election forever changed me. I got the staggering correlation between election fraud and mining the Penokee Hills. Falling into the Election Integrity movement saved my life. These heroic activists educated me on the history of election fraud and helped move through my own shock and awe. As I came to grips with the years of fraud, voting machine scandals, corruption and deceit on all levels of our election systems, something kicked on inside me.

Reform takes leaders willing to call out the injustices and offer solutions. I knew that was the only answer for me: to use my gifts to help Wisconsin. If we can save Wisconsin from this takeover, I thought, maybe we could set a precedent for the rest of the country. And yet, how could I imagine that the Election Integrity movement in Wisconsin could do what no other Election Integrity movement has been able to do in Florida and Ohio?

First, *because* we are Wisconsin. If you live here, you know what I mean. If you don't, I hope you're getting an idea. Wisconsin is and always has been a leader in reform, change and creating systems that serve the whole. For years, Republicans, Democrats and Progressives have worked together to govern and legislate a state worth living in. We pride ourselves on politicians being servants, and citizens being responsible, educated and contributing back to society. We take seriously our stewardship of the Earth and aren't afraid to stand up for it and each other.

And here we were, in the right place, at the right time, with the momentum of history at our backs. The Supreme Court race forced the recount that revealed the corruption and fraud right before nine recall elections were about to be held. As observers, we knew we had to take action to protect the summer recalls.

The Summer of Recalls

After Prosser was waved back onto the bench, he immediately overturned the lower court's ruling on violation of open meetings law and the Republicans marched on. Calling two "Extraordinary Sessions" to begin fast-tracking passage of their ALEC-inspired bills, they restricted our Constitutional rights, dismantled education and the environment, bankrupted our poor communities and protected the rich ones. And once again, abusing their majority power, they enacted one of the most restrictive voter suppression bills in the country as well as conducting, again behind closed doors, an expensive and secretive redistricting process, paid for by the taxpayers—all designed to keep voters from the polls.

However, We the People were hard at work as well. The State pulled together thousands of volunteers and quickly gained enough legitimate names to bring six Republicans to the polls for special elections later in the summer. Republicans just barely succeeded in pulling the Democrats into the recall fray by hiring out-of-state rabble-rousers to collect names for them.[79] These right-wing operatives working in Dave Hansen's district actually told petitioners that they were signing a form that *supported* Hansen. Other illegal tactics were used, and the GAB was forced to eliminate several of the GOPs efforts, leaving three Democrats vulnerable to losing their seats in the recalls.

The observers from the recount watched, drawn together by our helplessness, knowing most of the state had no idea the level of election fraud that was taking place, much less the depth and breadth of corruption in the voting system itself. How in the world would we protect the recalls? As a group of whistle-blowers, we were terrified that the Republicans and their corporate sponsors would steal these elections in the same way they stole the Supreme Court seat. To keep their majority power, Republicans needed to defend at least four of their six seats.

Now that we knew how they could be stealing the votes, the stakes were higher. If Walker lost the legislature, surely heads would roll. Already he was far behind his other brethren governors who had secured their states' takeovers early on. Synder was expanding financial martial law in Michigan and had stripped elected officials in Benton Harbor of all their power. The heat was on the Wisconsin Republicans to game the system at all costs.

The observers quickly took action. One group splintered off and became Wisconsin Citizens for Election Protection (WCEP). Guided in part by two former clerks from Middleton, a plan was put into place to work with the county clerks to convince them to do hand counts and allow us to observe. This is when we discovered the law prevented hand counts for municipalities over 7500 without express permission of the GAB. The good news was, two municipalities, Merrill and Tomahawk, had already written for and had been granted permission to do hand counts.

79 http://www.politiscoop.com/us-politics/wisconsin-politics/past-news-stories/207-Republicans-now-hiring-out-of-state-felons-canvasser-arrested-in-crime-spree.html

AMERICANS FOR PROSPERITY®
WISCONSIN

Dear [redacted]

Important State Senate Recall Election in your area soon!

Enclosed, please find an application for an absentee ballot. As a member of Americans for Prosperity who lives in a district where one of the eight **state senate recall elections** are taking place in **August 2011**, we wanted to make it as easy as possible for you and one other person in your home to vote.

Please follow the 4-step process:

> **Step 1:** Fill out the attached application for an absentee ballot today (be sure to sign the application).
>
> **Step 2:** Mail your application to: Absentee Ballot Application Processing Center, P.O. Box 1327, Madison, WI 53701-1327.
>
> **Step 3:** When you receive your absentee ballot from your city clerk, fill it out immediately.
>
> **Step 4:** Mail in your completed absentee ballot which must be received by your city clerk on the Thursday of the week before the general election (your clerk will provide more instructions)

If you intend to apply for the absentee ballot to vote, please fill out the application and mail it today

More so than ever before, the control of the State Senate is in your hands. I strongly encourage you to vote early and let your voice be heard.

Thank you,

Matt Seaholm,

State Director

1126 S 70th Street, Suite S219A, Milwaukee, WI 53214
Phone: (414) 476-7900 | Fax: (414) 476-2800 | www.americansforprosperit

Koch-funded Americans for Prosperity mailed out false information to Democrats during the Summer 2011 recall elections. The return address to send the absentee ballot application to was that of the Wisconsin Family Action Pac, an arm of Right to Life. The statement that voters had to get their ballots back to their clerks at least one week before the election was false, as they had until the end of election day to return them. Major media picked up this story, but one more thing for which AFP, Right to Life and Wisconsin Family Action Pac will never be held accountable.

Working with the clerks, WCEP organized and trained volunteers to be ready to observe at the polls after they closed. WCEP people would document the condition of ballot bags and touchscreen poll tapes, video how the votes were counted and sealed, where they went and how they arrived the next day at the clerks' offices. This Herculean effort was largely overshadowed by the Get Out The Vote (GOTV) and canvassing efforts. All the while I thought uneasily, why waste your time getting out the votes if they end up stealing them anyway? But in truth we needed every effort on every front to beat this multi-level assault on our election systems over the long haul.

Another group splintered off to become Election Defense Alliance of Wisconsin, part of the national EDA, an umbrella organization for Election Integrity groups across the country that formed after the 2004 presidential steal. Working with the magazine *Wisconsin Wave,* EDAW trained and organized exit polls for Senate District 8, where Sandy Pasch, a no-nonsense Democrat unafraid to speak the truth, was closely chasing Republican Alberta Darling. SD8 would be the most likely place for the theft, given Darling's devotion to ALEC, the takeover, and her high standing in the Republican food chain. All of us decided to give SD8 a little extra attention.

Meanwhile the Republicans and Tea Partiers were working hard to suppress the vote. Republicans decided to redistrict, in secret, hiring a law firm that was charging the taxpayers $395 an hour, without any input from the Democrats. Their map basically slanted the entire state for the red and cost the taxpayers nearly $500,000. Americans For Prosperity was mailing out absentee ballot applications to the opposition with the wrong dates for the elections. Wisconsin Right to Life robo-calls also targeted Democrats. [See a list of illegal activities in Attachments Part II, appendix.]

After the smoke cleared, eight primaries and nine elections later, the Democrats kept all three of their seats and gained two, but Wisconsin watched, election night, right before our eyes as once again the seat they needed most was in question. Watching the live coverage at the Majestic Theater, the Democratic headquarters in downtown Madison, I almost threw up when word came that Kathy Nickolaus was going to delay releasing the results of Senate District 8, Alberta Darling, maybe even until the morning.

Chaos erupted at the Majestic when MSNBC reporter Ed Shultz, broadcasting live from the square, said the name, *Kathy Nickolaus.* Even the lay people understood they had been punked again.

The crowd that night was furious. So many had worked so hard to make this historic moment possible. That once again Democracy was in the hands of Kathy Nickolaus was maddening. Democratic Chairman Mike Tate raged out to the podium, demanding that someone, anyone, look into election fraud. He publicly accused Nickolaus of once again gaming the elections, a statement he later retracted, more than likely for legal protection. However, his words were heard across the state, and as outraged as I was, I was secretly relieved that his outburst carried the words *election fraud* across national news—one more media moment of truth.

Although we did not completely bring back checks and balances to our house, the victories from the summer recalls later led to the defeat of the mining bill and brought us one small step closer. Wisconsin was proving to be exactly what we claimed: a citizenry that will never stand down, one that will protect our Democracy at all costs.

Open Pit Iron Ore Mine

Through it all, I was also monitoring the progress of the propaganda campaign being launched by G-Tac, which held the mineral rights to hundreds of acres of the Penokee Hills in the north of the state. Representatives for the mines had up until now been holding public meetings to educate us on their intentions, *(jobs, jobs, jobs)* and assured us that they would do "responsible" mining and abide by the Wisconsin rules and regulations in place to protect the environment.

After Walker was elected, their tone changed dramatically; suddenly these restrictions were too onerous for them to obey, and if we wanted their *jobs, jobs, jobs* we would have to loosen up Wisconsin's environmental safeguards. However, when asked how much water their mine would be using, we were told that information was "proprietary." Soon it became clear: legislators being sponsored by the mines were allowing the mining companies to write the mining legislation. A draft of their proposed bill was leaked in May 2011. It stripped away all safeguards for the environment, removing any recourse for the people, land and water potentially damaged by the mines, and contained absolutely no expectation of accountability from G-Tac. The bill was so awful and the political climate of Wisconsin so divisive that the Republicans pulled the bill before the summer recalls to table until the Fall. Rightfully concerned that the extreme measure would harm their already sinking public image further, the Republicans turned their focus onto the recalls.

By September 2011 environmental activists from around the state came together to organize an educational campaign to protect the Penokee Hills and water from this destruction. The Bad River Band of Lake Superior Chippewa came out early with a resolution opposed to the mine and stating their clean water standards. As the biggest employer in the area, they provided millions of dollars in taxes, revenue and employment while also serving as stewards for the protection of the land. Executive Order 39 confirmed their right to co-manage the ceded territory around the reservation. The potential destruction of a 22-mile mountaintop removal open pit iron ore mine was not worth the risk; the Bad River watershed was essential to the balance of the area's entire ecosystem. If mining were to proceed, the runoff of sulfide pollution would flow right through their land and into our the water table, destroy their wild rice beds and eventually pollute fish, wildlife and humans as it made its way to Lake Superior.

Also at play was the fact that Wisconsin had received a grant to develop wind power, an initiative that would create hundred of new jobs and was the product of years of research and negotiation by sustainability groups. With the stroke of the pen, Walker changed the regulations concerning wind farms, making it impossible for them to do business, successfully removing any competition for the mines, and now was able to claim the need for mines to provide jobs.

Meanwhile, in Chippewa County, residents had been fighting the sand frac mining companies for over a year. These deadly operations spread a fine white dust called silica, a highly-carcinogenic substance that has proven to cause health risks to humans and vegetation while polluting the ground water and soil. As soon as summer arrived, out-of-state frac companies began buying up farmland and putting up operations at lightning speed. Almost overnight, rural roads where Amish carriages and bicyclists traveled were now carrying 15 trucks an hour, traveling at top speed, 18 hours a day, six days a week. The area began to resemble the surface of the moon, as the deadly dust endangered residents' lives, closed local businesses, and decreased property values, while the *jobs, jobs, jobs* turned out to be

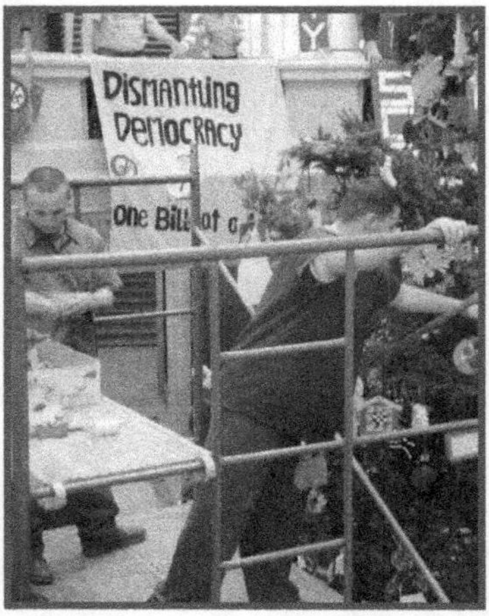

Christmas 2011, Wisconsin State Capitol. Walker chose to not pay state workers to decorate the tree and instead shipped in prison labor to do the job for free. Many believe he would use them for mining jobs. Photo: Rebecca Kemble

funneled through temporary employment agencies. Many soon feared Walker's plan was eventually to use prison inmates and do away with the last of whatever benefit the mines were to provide economically. Later in the year, these fears came to pass as Walker used prison labor to decorate the Capitol holiday tree, which he renamed a "Christmas" tree.

Violations of First Amendment Rights

According to statute 19:90, Wisconsin citizens are free to videotape the proceedings of our state government. However, the Assembly took up a rule that said otherwise and tried to make it illegal for us to videotape them. We the People believed our Constitution trumped the rules of the Assembly, for our own protection, especially under these trying circumstances.

> *WI Statute 19.90 Use of equipment in open session. Whenever a governmental body holds a meeting in open session, the body shall make a reasonable effort to accommodate any person desiring to record, film or photograph the meeting. This section does not permit recording, filming or photographing such a meeting in a manner that interferes with the conduct of the meeting or the rights of the participants.*

On October 25, 2011, I was present in the Assembly for a nonviolent action orchestrated by concerned citizens being denied their Constitutional rights. For months people had been ticketed for holding a protest sign, only to go to court and have the charge dismissed. On this night, a man was handcuffed for wearing a lanyard with a cross on it with the words "love sign." One woman was harassed because her sign was sewn to her shirt. I witnessed pages instructing people holding copies of the Constitution that they could not hold them with the printed page facing the Assembly, however, they could hold them if the printed page faced them, as if they were reading. I witnessed the indiscriminate targeting of certain citizens but not others, as two people were allowed to use their cell phones openly in the gallery while others were made to stop. I saw some citizens dragged out for holding a sign, and others, like myself, were not. I saw people silently videotaping told to stop, and when they quietly and respectfully stated the Constitutional statute that allowed them to do so, were taken out of the gallery and arrested, only to later be released with a ticket for disturbing the peace, which later did not hold up in court.

As peaceful protesters were forcibly handcuffed and hauled out of the gallery to the basement, it was clear that more peace was disturbed and costs were incurred by the Republicans' attempt to stifle free speech using State Patrol (sometimes 12 at a time in the gallery) than any of the protesters standing up for the 1st Amendment.

That night, Rep. Pocan and the Democrats put forth the resolution to bring the wind power grant back to the table. This bill would immediately provide economic relief to 171 businesses across the state. Wisconsin was poised to begin building wind farms, creating 1,000 new jobs in a sustainable energy field. I watched as the Republicans refused to bring the bill out of committee. Their only response was that they would work with the Democrats, at some time, but not now.

But why not? I believe because Republicans were serving the corporate interests of Koch and Cline Mines, any kind of sustainable energy would be unwelcome competition for the big profits they were eyeing via mining, sand fracking, and oil exploration. The Republicans had the audacity to turn down a bill that would have provided economic stimulus and sustainable energy in this time of needed resources, thereby successfully doing the bidding of their corporate sponsors. For me, this was another RICO action.

On this night, the Republicans brought forth bill after bill that had nothing to do with helping the economy—honoring pregnancy centers; allowing fairgrounds to serve wine; making sure felons can't possess a vicious dog; and one of my favorites, a bill that successfully prevents a town from holding a multiple martial arts contest. As the fascists once again lock-step extortion voted whatever they were told, the Assembly Democrats had a plan.

Around 8:30 PM they went into caucus and emerged with a resolution to protect our the First Amendment rights. Rep. Pocan read the resolution that would support the Constitution and the right of citizens to hold a sign and videotape in the gallery.

When asked who would co-sponsor the resolution, all the Democrats stepped up in the show of solidarity to protect our rights. Rep. Hebl (D-Sun Prairie) actually read a passage from Alexander Solzhenitsyn's scorching epic about totalitarianism, *Gulag Archipelago*, in a plea to get the Republicans to see the error of their fascist ways.[80] For the first time that night, the Republicans, usually in-different, busy texting, checking their Facebook pages, or talking amongst themselves, sat silent. What could they say when their fellow legislators pointed out that they were traitors in the act of committing treason?

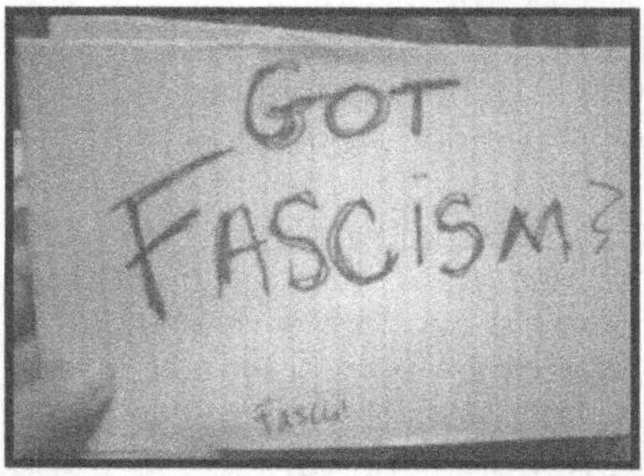

During this, I was allowed to sit in the front of the gallery holding my impromptu creation, "Got Fascism?" Believe you me, every single Republican got my hairy eyeball, my steely stare meant to burn through the propaganda they were using to collectively create their false reality. My message was, "The emperor has no clothing, and we all know it."

In the end, the Republicans voted to table the 1st Amendment resolution, successfully demonstrating that not only would they *not* stand up for our Constitutional rights, but the following morning, the State Patrol presence was doubled, and the Senate Republicans also took up a resolution to *stifle* free speech in that gallery. In this way, both houses had now fallen to fascism.

Recall Walker

On November 19, 2011 citizen Julie Wells filed the official recall papers for Scott Walker. Throughout the next two months of circulating recall petitions in the middle of winter, countless volunteers gathered over 990,000 signatures to recall the governor. Another 800,000 were collected for the recall of Lt. Gov. Rebecca Kleefisch, and another 80,000 for

80 http://www.youtube.com/watch?v=NHfm-C1oRwg

November 4, 2011. Dane County Courthouse. Some of the heroes who stood up to the illegal rules the fascists were trying to impose to limit our free speech and freedom to petition the government our grievances. After getting their day in court, all charges were dismissed. From left: Attorney Jim Mueller, Whitney and Kathy Steffan, Mary Jo Walters, Joseph Skulan, Jason Huberty, Thi Li, Harriett Rowan, Paul Schmid, CJ Terrell and Emily Hoppe.

four more Republican senators. This action demonstrated that out of 5 million eligible voters, almost 2 million votes were collected to remove these fascists from office, representing over one-third of the state.

Despite the propaganda circulated by the fascists, this statement was by and large the greatest tribute to citizen participation in Democracy the country has seen in recent years. As Wisconsin stood on the precipice of what we dubbed *The Mother of All Recall Elections*, and the John Doe investigation circled closer to Walker himself, one signature at a time, We the People prevailed.

More Violation of Constitution and Open Meeting Law

On January 26, 2012, Wisconsin Assembly Speaker Pro Tem Rep. Bill Kramer (R-ALEC) ordered all observers removed from the gallery and behind locked doors conducted the passage of AB426, the ALEC-G-Tac-authored ferrous mining bill.[81] Despite a majority of opposition at both public hearings, stripping away all protections from air, water and people, removing contested case hearings, violating the Great Lakes Compact and Federal Treaty Rights, and putting the Bad River Indians at risk of genocide (among

81 http://wcmcoop.com/members/wi-assembly-Republicans-violate-article-iv-section-10-of-the-wi-consitution-and-illegally-pass-ab426/

many other despicable aspects of the bill), the Republican fascists once again colluded to use their majority to do the bidding of their corporate sponsors: Cline Mines, G-Tac, ALEC, Caterpillar, to name a few. At the same time, they violated Article IV, Section 10 of the Wisconsin Constitution that requires the doors of the legislator to remain open:

> *Journals; open doors; adjournments.* Section *10. Each house shall keep a journal of its proceedings and publish the same, except such parts as require secrecy. The doors of each house shall be kept open except when the public welfare shall require secrecy. Neither house shall, without consent of the other, adjourn for more than three days.*

January 26, 2012, the night AB426 was passed illegally when the doors to the Assembly were locked, and the Republicans violated Article IV, Section 10 of the Wisconsin Constitution and Wisconsin Open Meeting Law. Photo: Michael Matheson

How We Stopped AB 426 is a story in and of itself. When we last saw them, G-Tac left the state abruptly after the bill died on the Senate floor, thanks to the vote of the same Republican who voted against the budget repair bill, Dale Schultz (R-New Richmond). He and Sen. Jauch spent time on the Bad River reservation and smoked out of the actual peace pipe that Chief Buffalo brought to Washington, DC in the 1800s. Shortly after that pow wow, the bill died on the floor and abruptly, Sen. Galloway, (R-Wausau) resigned as of immediately. This left the Senate now tied and brought another small step toward restoring checks and balances.

Stealing the Recall

The next round of recall elections were held on June 5, 2012. This was predictably the classic stolen election from the start:

voting machine trade-outs all across the state;[82] the already installed hackable machines; the millions Walker spent on propaganda ads; the illegal robo-calls informing people that if they signed the recall petition they did not have to vote;[83] the collusion with the media who called Walker the winner 45 minutes after the polls closed with only 21% of the precincts reporting; and the known corruption in Waukesha. There was no question in any of the minds of the election integrity leaders around the country that this was a steal. Many feel this was part of preparing the nation for the steal of the Presidential election in November 2012.[84]

Part of heating the water slowly under the pot full of frogs.

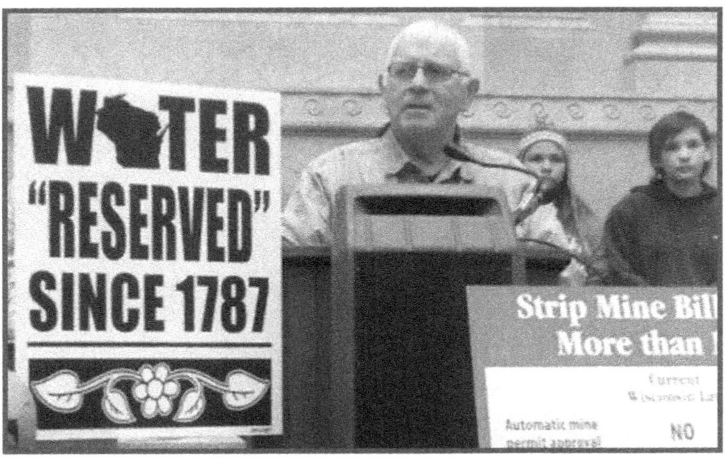

January 26, 2011. Elder Joe Rose, member of the Bad River Band of the Lake Superior Chippewa Indians speaking at a press conference at the Capitol: "We entered the seventh fire about 30 years ago. The first steps taken on Earth were done with love, honor and respect ... What is our meaning and purpose as humans? It's simple: we were put here to live in harmony with all of creation and to never take more than what we need. It's complex: We are caught in the web of life with ecosystems and interrelationships with other living things ... We are undergoing a paradigm shift from values based on money and political power to the new times where wealth is measured in clean water, fresh air and pristine wilderness. Anishinaabe have been given the responsibility to share the knowledge of how to live in harmony with creation." Photo: Rebecca Kemble

82 http://wcmcoop.com/members/meet-command-central-the-people-in-charge-of-wisconsin-voting-machines/
83 http://articles.latimes.com/2012/jun/05/news/la-pn-voter-suppressing-robocalls-reported-in-wisconsin-recall-20120605
84 http://www.youtube.com/watch?v=Dc8ZiPw-Z1Q

The Wisconsin Revolution is not about unions, the budget, collective bargaining or our environment. It's about the stealing of the process of democracy to install legislators and court justices who will break the law to take control of all of our resources. All those issues are just casualties of these crimes.

"Justice," Wisconsin State Capitol

CALL TO ACTION

Modern US Revolution

Never before in modern history has the United States been faced with such a far-reaching attempt to instigate a hostile takeover of the government. Politicians in all parties are turning their backs on their oath of office and their duty to protect the Constitution when they pass rules, statutes, and "laws" that benefit the corporations at the expense of the earth, the people and the process of Democracy. Local papers run propaganda pieces penned by Koch-funded organizations like MacIver Institute[85] and Wisconsin Policy Research Institute[86] as if they were real news agencies. Judges continue to pave the way for elimination of human rights and protecting the guilty.

In November 2011, both the US Senate and the House passed a bill that would allow US citizens to be detained indefinitely for no reason.[87] Here in Wisconsin, our rights are also being stripped from us and our resources drained. Wisconsin Republicans have been lock-step extortion-voting ALEC legislation at a frightening pace while state troopers

85 http://www.sourcewatch.org/index.php?title=MacIver_Institute

86 http://thinkprogress.org/politics/2011/02/21/145492/zombie-johnbirch-walker/

87 http://www.huffingtonpost.com/2011/12/01/military-detention-us-citizens-senate-second-vote_n_1123929.html

arrest us for exercising our Constitution rights. It is our duty, now more than ever, to participate in, observe and document what our public officials are up to.

Fascism is privatized government manipulated by the wealthy that intentionally uses its strength to silence the voice of the people to forcibly suppress opposition and criticism. Using judicial, election, and legislative systems to regulate industry to benefit their own needs at the expense of the many, the fascists then use the media propaganda echo chamber to broadcast lies and propaganda as tools of suppression. These are the totalitarians—corporations, banksters, big oil and mining cartels, voting machine manufacturers, corrupt politicians at all levels of government. They are attempting to create a centralized, privatized police state that will not tolerate opinions differing from theirs as to exercise dictatorial control over every aspect of our lives.

In a corporate hostile takeover, the overpowering entity purposefully attempts to devalue the competition so they can buy them up at rock-bottom prices. In this case, the "competition" is the government, and the ALEC-affiliated legislators are the tools to install the system to make government fail from the inside out. Their goal is to pass laws that will bankrupt local towns and counties, so that they will then claim the need to "take control"—declare financial martial law as they have in Michigan—"for our own good." In reality, it's been the fascists in power creating the poor conditions to begin with, for this very end.

After all the banks own all the foreclosed homes, the corporatists are free to purchase the land for next to nothing.

Fascism differs from other forms of oligarchy in that its value system is completely devoid of ethics. One can resist a theocracy—a purely God-driven government—by exposing the immorality of the regime. A state with abusive public servants can also be exposed. Citizen activism can even resist an oppressor of Democratic principles by clearly demonstrating the violations of rights.

Fascism, however, is fiercely intent in its pursuit of total control on every level of rule. Its success is measured by a triumph of might over everything and everyone, at all costs. What the fascists consider "strong," the rest of civil society deems immoral. It's also why resisting this modern-day fascist takeover with righteousness cannot be the only step to overturning the regime.

When addressing the protests in Wisconsin March 2011, Michael Moore explained: Most good people can't fathom the psychology of such evil and therefore underestimate the threat of fascism. "It can't happen here" is a common response, because good people *want* to have faith in others, especially their government. After all, if your government betrays you, where can you turn? It's the most frightening kind of terrorism there is. The more we understand the depth of emotional stress we are under as we are assaulted with multiple fronts, the better able we can transform the effects of *shock and awe* into *effective nonviolent action* to reclaim Democracy.

Hate Is Their Tool

Fascism appeals to the fringes of society and provides people who are normally deviant a way to participate that feeds their subversive obsessions. As tools of hate, they are given a focus—liberals, Obama, immigrants, environmentalists, teachers, unions, gays, Native Americans—on which to aim their subversions. Their passion is fulfilled by being sanctioned to take action to destroy what they think is their enemy.

Cyber War

Provocateurs called *cyber-trolls* are specially trained to launch continuous online attacks against grassroots activists supporting peace and justice. Teams of trolls are paid to search publications for articles that reveal the truth and add hateful, discrediting propaganda in the comment boxes. Multiple posting by the same troll can create the illusion of support for their hate when in truth it's a small handful with several accounts being paid and protected by the corporate interests. Activists can easily get banned from posting on their own Facebook accounts through the efforts of the trolls, but the pages filled with hate, urging people to take illegal action, stay up for months, despite repeated complaints sent to Facebook and law enforcement.

One troll strategy on Facebook is to report everything an activist posts as spam, purposefully getting them suspended. Even further, they have taken to publishing home addresses, phone numbers and personal information of activists on the web, as well as regular death threats. Because of this, I recommend using Facebook to move information among allies, not as a battleground for these thugs. Engaging on any level is wasted time. Report their threatening and illegal activities to law enforcement to have a record of the abuse. Then keep yourself safe. The lies will speak for themselves.

Without dissent, they become hollow clanging in the empty echo chamber of their own propaganda.

Shock and Awe is designed to render people incapable of resistance. That is the end goal of hate as well: to inspire us to hate them back, thereby diverting our attention from the effective action we should be taking to defend ourselves. Hate will take us down, too, if we become like them. Take the high road and ignore the hate messages. See them merely as expressions of their own hate—a hate that is ultimately destroying them from within. Stand up for justice; stand back from hate.

Anger, however, can be channeled into taking direct action to restore justice. Hate and anger are natural emotions, but it is vital to the nonviolent movement that we don't use them to destroy our enemies, but instead let them fuel our civic duty to stand against the injustices that are destroying us. It is human to cry out in anguish as you see the world you treasure and value being dismantled for greed; but our anguish must not prevent us from taking actions that promote the solidarity of the decency and common good.

Restoring Checks and Balances

When the founding mothers and fathers wrote the Constitution and the Bill of Rights, they knew an American despot could arise. They came to America *because* of living through tyranny. Their intention was to create a place safe from that oppression. This is the purpose of checks and balances; they are required for this radical vision of self-determination—Democracy—to succeed. Human nature will abuse power if power is left unchecked. I believe good citizens, once they process the shock and awe, *want* to protect the Constitution. It's our governmental compass designed to administer justice for the good of the whole Republic, not just the richest few.

The founders did not intend for us to delegate the defense of liberty. If we ever got to this place of American tyranny, they intended for us to take action to defend our nation. Their vision was not big enough to see all of us here in 2012, but was sound enough to impel every individual—the ordinary people—to assume the patriotic task and stand up to restore Democracy. We must learn to channel the founders' faith in us and stand up in this extraordinary experiment they began over 200 years ago.

We the People are part of the checks and balances. Protecting Wisconsin from fascism will require the participation of as many people as possible on as many levels as possible. The personal challenge for each individual will be in knowing what action to take that will be effective. How do you as an individual take action to protect your rights, your natural resources and your vote? Especially in the face of such seemingly overwhelming odds?

Become The Change

One of the first steps to regain our republic is to learn to process the emotion around what's happening. There's a reason they call it *shock and awe.* The devastation is meant to be so immediate and far-reaching that your mind and heart can literally go into shock and become unable to take action. Witnessing such evil sends average humans into denial as a survival response.

While observing at the recount in Waukesha and seeing bag after bag of ballots with broken chains of custody, I felt numb. The possible crime seemed too large to address and too horrific to acknowledge. That a mining company was allowed to write the mining laws is so absurd that a part of my mind shuts down. Pondering the absurdity of ALEC creates a vacuum. The key to reconnecting is acknowledging and releasing the emotion behind the denial. We must learn to process the shock in an effective, nonviolent fashion in order to take action.

So how we do constructively move through this emotional blitzkrieg? What are effective steps to redirect the shock and awe into effective action? We must find a way to honor our deep and justifiable anger, anxiety and feelings of powerlessness, and channel that into direct, powerful, nonviolent action. All of us together then become a force.

#1 Accept this is Real: Feel and Breathe

As you discover the truth of the takeover, allow yourself a moment to accept it. "Accepting" means honoring all the emotions that go along with that truth. Fear, rage, despair, anxiety—these are the emotions meant to *shock and awe* you into inaction. When you deny the takeover is real because it's too frightening to admit, you suppress the fear in order to feel safe, thereby not taking action to stand against it. This is the desired outcome of those administering the shock and awe.

Repressing or denying the feeling of shock and awe, in the end, is the danger. It keeps you asleep and unprepared to deal with the situation most effectively. By embracing the emotions behind the truth instead of denying them, you literally move the shock wave through your body like electricity. By doing so you can break the spell of awe, and move forward to take action for the good of all.

When you become scared or anxious, take a short time-out to process the emotion. Wherever you are, take several long, slow breaths in and out to process the shock wave of whatever arises. Try to stop your intellect from telling yourself a story about *why* you are feeling this. As you breathe, mindfully pull the pure essence of the real *emotion* through your body with your breath. Repeat as needed. Literally breathing the emotion through your body will prevent denial and pave the way for action.

Think of it as Emotional Yoga. This small but repeated action can help prevent those difficult and painful emotions from building up and causing you to take impulsive action that might not be for your own best interest as well as the interest of your cause.

Think of it like this: if you live in a tornado alley, you don't avoid knowing what to do if a tornado strikes. You face the fear ahead of time and put precautions in place to be prepared if, heaven forbid, you should have to experience such a disaster. The more you deny the possibility, the less prepared and more afraid you are on that stormy night.

The more you face the truth of the hostile takeover, the better prepared you will be to take action. Spend some time safely releasing the emotion. Kick, scream, cry, then hide under your covers for a while. Curse the bastards then remember the years you lived in denial and contributed to the conflict by not paying attention yourself. Wonder, as we all did when we were facing our own shock and awe, how did the United States get into this condition? Now we know.

As you look at the challenge of restoring the Republic straight in the eye, the good news is, millions of people around the world are standing right there with you, embracing their own lives as they, too, are waking up to take action. You are now a part of a force of nature that's been building for a long time. You will meet many people who have been waiting for you. Naomi Wolf, author of *The End of America,* was one of my guides. I stumbled upon her book at the beginning of the Wisconsin revolution, and with her help I was able to wake up and smell the fascism.

Once you accept the truth, it is your duty as a citizen of the United States to stand up and take action.

2# Commit To Nonviolence: Become the Change
Once you accept and expect the insanity of the situation, I advocate for a commitment to nonviolence. I suggest we even sign pledges of intention like the one in the back of this book (p. 116). Because we are one society of humans, we must learn to make decisions for the good of the whole. This is because a wound to one is a wound to all. By committing to nonviolent change, we access our real power by honoring and protecting the whole as a part of us. This change we are hoping to instigate in the world—be it political, environmental, spiritual or economic—must begin within each of us. Working for peace means a commitment to become a channel for that peace by continued self-awareness of how our own decisions are impacting the whole.

Violence: An unjust or unwarranted exertion of force or power, as against rights or laws; swift and intense force.

Nonviolence: Absence of exertion of physical force that injures or abuses.

Civil Disobedience/Civic Duty: The obligation to refuse to obey certain governmental demands as unjust and in violation of individual and environmental rights, for the purpose of influencing legislation, government and judicial policy, characterized by the employment of such nonviolent techniques as boycotting, picketing, singing protest songs, education campaigns and any other way to keep the focus on the injustice and debunk the lies of their propaganda.

The Challenges of Nonviolence
Those who believe "might is right" will paint nonviolence as a weak response to an overwhelming challenge. The illegal, unjust and violent responses the police and government are perpetrating may leave us feeling all is lost and thinking that we, too, have to resort to those extreme tactics. However, perpetrating violence means we become a channel for violence, as we extort force and abuse over those doing the abusing. An eye for an eye will make the entire world blind.

In 1957, Martin Luther King wrote a piece called *The Power of Nonviolence.*[88] In it, he explains that when he first brought the concept to his community, many rejected it as cowardice. It took many meetings and education about the idea of nonviolent resistance to convey the power behind the action. The nonviolent resisters are attacking the evil system of fascism, not destroying the individuals who are perpetrating it. The idea is to stand strong for justice rather than against one group of people. In King's case, his mission was not to address the struggle between blacks and whites, but to affect a victory for a Democracy that says, "All men are created equal."

He also espoused the notion that this is equally an internal struggle, wherein each individual must come to understand his or her personal power. Changing first from within, each person will make the overall societal change more powerful. When we understand our own impact, and dedicate ourselves to making decisions for the good of the whole of society, change will become lasting.

While we all seek to live a well-adjusted life free from neurosis and imbalance, King felt there is a type of necessary "maladjustment" needed to accomplish our goal to overthrow the fascists. We must never "adjust" ourselves to accept discrimination and the abuse of our rights. We must never become accustomed to unjust violence against us from our own government. King's words were, "God grant that we will be so maladjusted that we will be able to go out and change our world and our civilization. And then we will be able to move from the bleak and desolate midnight of man's inhumanity to man to the bright and glittering daybreak of freedom and justice."[89]

Nonviolence vs. Self-Defense

Some believe that violence may be needed in order to defend oneself. The 2nd Amendment gives us the right to bear arms, precisely because our Founders knew too well how government-controlled militia could be used to do the bidding of the despots. The past ten years have seen a change in laws that now allow for illegal search and seizure as part of the Patriot Act. There is now a law that allows the US to detain American citizens without cause, indefinitely.[90] The decision whether to remain nonviolent, or, as the

88 http://teachingamericanhistory.org/library/index.asp?document=1131

89 *The Power of Nonviolent*, Martin Luther King, June 4, 1957.

90 http://rt.com/usa/news/indefinite-detention-bill-senate-905/

Constitution allows, take up arms to protect ourselves when our rights are being suppressed, is indeed a complex question that every individual must decide for his or herself.

At the Occupy Wall Street movement, disenfranchised veterans showed up to protect the protesters from police violence armed only with their uniforms and powerful voices. But in 1964, a group of African American men in Louisiana created an armed self-defense organization called the Deacons for Defense and Justice. They provided protection for workers from the police who were targeting them with violence and became a rallying point for a militant working-class movement in the South. In a similar but nonviolent fashion, Occupiers are lending their force now to stand up for the disenfranchised, for example, occupying the homes of neighbors being unfairly foreclosed upon.

Self-defense is an art that is best used fluidly, depending on each individual situation. However, the odds are greater that you will create a nonviolent outcome if you are committed to nonviolence. Attacks on Occupy Wall Street's unarmed resistors would only have escalated if fire had been returned and people on both sides would have renounced the entire movement. Making this oath strengthens the will during those moments when self-defense is needed against gross abuses of power. It also forces more creative, action-oriented solutions, such as creating a citizen media co-op to report the truth, or conducting a daily sing-along where people can gather strength, news and inspiration together.

How self-defense manifests must be the choice of each individual. Regardless of your views, this author recommends nonviolent resistance.

#3 Educate Yourself

Turn off corporate media and research on your own. Join Facebook and watch it happen live. Watch the Wiseye.org videos of our politicians and see first hand what they are doing with the power we gave them. Better yet, occupy the State Assembly and Senate and watch your government live in action. Read Wisconsin Citizens Media Coop regularly.[91] Cultivate critical thinking and take time to discover what's really going on. When you witness for yourself bills being passed using lock-step, rapid-fire extortion voting, something will change in you, I guarantee.

---

91 http://wcmcoop.com/members/

Understanding the Nature of Evil Through Critical Thinking
Standing nonviolently in the face of evil can be exhausting. Most people aren't evil and have difficulty understanding how anyone could be so greedy that they would prefer to destroy others than do what's best for the whole. The insanity of destroying the Earth for profit is impossible to grasp. Facing and transforming the fear and terror of what appears to be the unstoppable force of fascism takes resilience, determination and courage. The good news is, these attributes a part of who you are and can be cultivated. Every time you take action, raise your voice and make a stand, you grow courage.

> **Evil:**
> Decisions made for the good of the few at the expense of the whole.
>
> **Peace and Justice:**
> Decisions made for the good of all.

Each time someone, anyone, stands up to exercise the rights that are being stolen, the power of the truth is embodied. No one "gives" you the right to free speech; it's just yours. As a human, you have a voice, and your voice has a right to be heard. That is why any small action to use your voice is much more powerful than the immediate result may reveal. That your letter to your fascist senator is answered with a canned response filled with lies does not mean your writing was a waste of time. Just the opposite: the more people who speak up in unity, the stronger each individual voice becomes.

Non-participatory government is no longer an option
You as a citizen are being charged with the responsibility to take action to protect your own individual rights, including the right to clean air and water, open government, free speech, to assemble and petition your government your grievances, and the right to vote in fair and open elections. If you don't take action, you leave your rights and your vote vulnerable to be stolen and used against you.

The Occupy Movement that spread around the world was in part seeded by the actions Wisconsin took in February 2011 and onward. This movement is a nonviolent resistance to demand what is rightfully ours: accountability from our elected officials to uphold their oath to protect us—our rights, our resources, and our Constitution. We seek justice for the thievery that has transpired with our pensions, mortgages, tax money, and public lands and water as the fascists intentionally bankrupt us as a part of the takeover. We demand protection for our human rights and natural resources, and from the endless wars being waged around the world with our tax dollars and labor.

Don't take my word for anything. Go find out for yourself. Use the links and references in this book. Develop an engagement in the world outside your own. Once you open your mind past the "tin hat conspiracy" rationale and see the truth, you will have just taken another step to become the change we need right now.

#4 Inspire Others to Educate Themselves
Repeatedly I have heard the question: How do we reach the archetypical, "My dad who watches Fox News?" Chances are, you and Dad either avoid talking politics, your tongue is nearly chewed off from biting it so much, or you repeatedly engage in one or two arguments that never lead anywhere. How can you find a new way to communicate with Dad to inspire him to wake up and educate himself?

Reaching out to friends and neighbors on the other side of the aisle is not as impossible as it might seem. First understand what category they fall into.

Good Citizens Being Lied To. This category includes Dad who watches Fox, and those citizens who still want to believe the government and the media would not betray us. They are in the denial that comes from wanting to believe the lies; the truth is too horrible to face. However, once they begin to learn for themselves, more often than not they become a powerful voice of resistance.

Wisconsin citizens woke up because they educated themselves on how the changes being instigated by the Walker administration would affect the state. It's the very reason the 14 Democrats went to Illinois: they were commanded to, in seven days, pass a budget that was designed to destroy the state. The Republicans made it clear: the Democrats had no choice. Leaving was the only way to give the people time to read it, too.

How many have yet to be affected, but will eventually get hit by these changes? Whether it's the smaller paychecks, the threat to their air and water, the sand frac mines going in across the State, the new draconian education "handbooks," getting thrown off Badgercare or the voting rolls—everyone in the state will eventually be personally impacted by the takeover. Approach your well-meaning but under-educated friends in a preemptive way. Lay the groundwork to help them understand your message.

Don't expect to instigate this conversation during one of your typical arguments. Make a point to have it when you aren't discussing politics. Plan it well. Tell your Dad you have a very important issue to discuss. Warn him, it's not an easy topic. Make him come and sit, then look him in the eye as you prepare to ask for his help.

Begin by affirming your common ground: your mutual love for Wisconsin and Democracy. Perhaps talking about the founding fathers, and how the Constitution wrote in a plan for if someone tried to overthrow the government.

Speak firsthand and from the heart. Don't argue or point fingers at Republicans. Steer the conversation away from political ideologies and onto defending Democracy. Just speak your truth: that you believe there is a hostile takeover of the government going on. Read from the Declaration of Independence. Tell him it's *your* duty to warn him and all Democracy-loving citizens: before it's too late, we must stand up and take action.

Share with him the violations of Constitutional rights that are being documented. Talk about the American Detention Bill. Show him footage of protesters being arrested for having pictures in the gallery. If he argues that they should not be there in the first place, try to explain that these are 1st Amendment Rights. These are the rights our veterans fought to protect. These brave activists are showing us what a police state the US has become. Tell him of your earnest fear that what has taken place in so many other countries around the world—Germany, Argentina, Cambodia, Russian—is now happening here.

However, in order to support him in developing critical thinking, you must allow him to process *his* shock and awe and discover the truth for himself. Don't argue. Tell him at this point that it's not your job to convince him. Your job is to inform him of his responsibilities and then point him in the right direction. Persuade him to educate himself. Give him jumping off points and ask him to just keep an open mind. Then step back and give him time.

Speaking from your heart and addressing your very real fears and the need to defend our Democracy is a much different tactic than attacking his TV habits or ideology. Talk about the assault on our rights and the environmental warfare. Introducing new language and perspectives may not be received instantly, but most people, when presented with the information in a direct and nonconfrontive way and then given space to process, will begin to consider the perspective, whether they want to or not.

Eventually, when people are advised and encouraged to look at what is happening as a hostile corporate takeover, they begin to understand. When they begin to see it for themselves, they will come looking for you, and you will be ready to help them find the right thing to do to take action.

Supporters of the Corporations. These are the deviants who support the fascist takeover, whether for personal profit or fear of an interruption to their comfort zone. With these people I suggest having prepared talking points. Remind them that this is not about liberals and conservatives, it's right or wrong, and that you are standing up for their rights, too. They, too, must come to understand the impact of their decisions, but do not make it at your expense. In the case of a closed mind, sometimes it's best to end the conversation and move along.

One of my oldest friends and next-door neighbor believes Walker is a saint, and says that any kind of charity is wrong, that poor people should be left to starve to death without health care or rights. In this case, I refuse to discuss politics with him, and while I still love him, I keep a healthy distance.

The fascists. These are the ones actually implementing the takeover. With this group, cutting through their propaganda echo chamber is vital to interjecting your will into their plans to steal Wisconsin. Telling it like it is at every turn is the best offense against the tools of fascism active in our government right now.

There is some discussion about the using the word, "fascist." By not shying away from this sometimes difficult term and in fact using it as a point of education, you send the signal that their lies fall on deaf ears, and that you will counter with the truth at every turn. "Fascist" is not a hate term; it's a grammatically correct use of the language to define someone who is engaged in the overthrow of the government. Also, it's one skill set to balance a budget; it's quite another to address fascism. The more we can address the real issue and not allow their lies to distract us, the more we can take effective actions to address the real issue.

The most important message you can send a fascist is that they will never intimidate you. Ever. Just because they say something is true does not make it so. Their own system is based on something for the good of the few at the expense of the many. They are by design self-destructive. Without the integrity of the whole, sooner or later they topple, and the will of the people once again reveals itself as the law of the land.

#5 Occupy Yourself: Take Action

Success depends on everyone standing up together for our rights. You are being called to educate yourself in order to restore peace and justice in your particular neighborhood/community/state/nation. Everywhere and on every level are opportunities to raise your voice, take action and make a difference. You get to choose what works for you, but nonetheless, you must take action. Learning how to best use your resources, and knowing you are making a difference will help determine what action you take.

End of the Nuclear Age

From a longer view, the world is being challenged to bring to a close what I call the *Nuclear Age,* one wherein war is seen as the unavoidable solution to conflict. Perhaps war was at one time a necessary evil, such as during World War II to stop the march of the Nazis. In 2012, however, we have war as a profit-making activity. With so much proliferation of nuclear weapons, smart bombs and chemical warfare in the hands of governments who cannot be trusted and passion-filled independent mercenaries, we are being challenged to transform society if only for the simple end goal of self-survival. War is no longer economically, environmentally or morally feasible. The next world war will probably be our last.

In 1955, Bertrand Russell read the final manifesto he and his friend Albert Einstein wrote together. Delivered several months after Einstein's death, the Russell Einstein Manifesto[92] spoke of the possibility of the termination of the entire human species and implored governments to seek peaceful means to resolve conflicts. Sounding more like psychics than scientists, the 11 signers knew how easily armed conflicts can escalate. Now that the world had nuclear weapons, the end game could result in massive, worldwide destruction.

What they did not see was how world economy would become intrinsically tied to war. The industrial war complex is draining the world of all valuable resources in the name of "security." Yet, my deepest fear is not some Arab/Muslim/Black terrorist threatening our country. I am far more terrified

92 http://barbarawith.com/RussellEinsteinManifesto.html

of corrupt state officials allowing elections to be stolen, and international mining companies taking our land to blow up our mountains to access ore to build more weapons for a never-ending war, now being waged against US citizens.

Regardless of your religious or spiritual beliefs, or lack thereof, the year 2012 has been heralded as a time of enormous change. Some believe these monolithic transformations are part of the evolution of the entire human species. As Einstein et al foresaw, we are at a crossroads. We either evolve into a species that cooperates in nonviolence and peace, or the world eventually kills itself with environmental warfare being perpetrated by the oil, mining, nuclear, coal and fossil fuel energy cartel that drives the industrial war complex. Equally complicit will be the millions of humans that continue to mindlessly support the system that rewards the corporations and is killing the planet.

Our secret weapon is our commitment: millions of individuals standing nonviolently to become the change. No surveillance team the fascists can construct will ever detect this tsunami of regenerative intention called *compassion*—people committed to making decisions for the good of the whole—of which all ordinary citizens are a part. There is no power greater than humans choosing to act out of concern for all. Knowing we are all one body, the union of human beings, means an act against one is an act against all. It also means each individual voice is imbued with the power of all.

In truth, we are far more dependent on water than money.

Studies have shown the groups, organizations, territories, communities, associations and individuals that commit to nonviolence foster more support than those that advocate for violence. Each individual must state his or her commitment to nonviolence, and then set about to find creative ways to channel that intention into action, sometimes in the face of gross injustice and evil. Standing strong together, committed to finding solutions nonviolently is the key for this reform to work. It is certainly why we're winning in Wisconsin.

GTAC
GOGEBIC TACONITE

March 6, 2012

Statement by Gogebic Taconite, LLC President Bill Williams on State Senate Rejection of Mining Reforms:

Senate rejection of the mining reforms in Assembly Bill 426 sends a clear message that Wisconsin will not welcome iron mining. We get the message. GTac is ending plans to invest in a Wisconsin mine. We thank the many people who have supported our efforts.

After months of assaulting us with lies, propaganda and secret government, including refusing to hear any bills on real job creation, the Republicans failed to pass their mining bill. We the People stood up and said no. In the end, it was a Republican, Dale Schultz, voting against it that killed it. So even though G-Tac paid to put Walker in office, had both the majority in the Assembly and Senate, full Executive support, was allowed to author the bill and ignore the voice of the people, they failed. This is their goodbye letter. The will of the people, when we stand up and exercise it, becomes the law of the land.

Conflict REVOLUTION

If we want our leaders to be accountable for their actions, we too must become accountable for ours. The nonviolent movement is more than anti-war; it's about finding new ways to coexist together on the Earth for self-preservation. Every facet of society is being challenged into awareness of the impact each citizen is leaving behind for seven generations to come. We must all reevaluate our carbon footprint, where we direct our energy, what we spend our money on, who we are supporting, where we put our time and connections, and how our communities interrelate.

To become the change, as Gandhi implored us, each person must ask himself or herself, "How might I unknowingly be propping up the corporate culture and affecting the planet adversely?"

How can each of us help usher in a new age of community, where nature and human rights are protected?

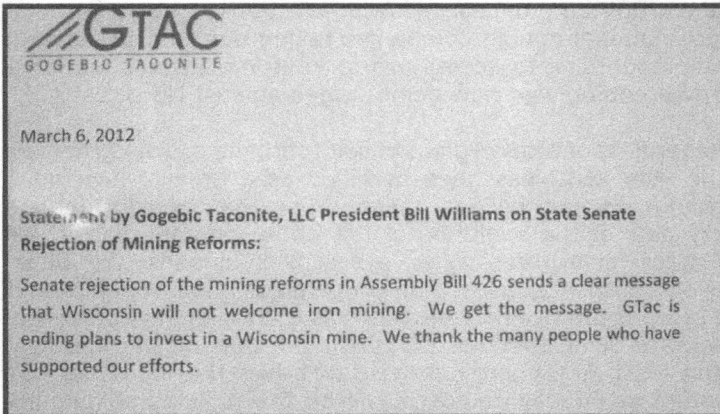

We must work to build communities from the ground up that are independent of the old system. For me, it's about disconnecting from the money-valued system, and working from a resources-valued system. This transition isn't easy; we have been fed the lie that we are dependent upon money. In reality, we are far more dependent upon clean air, clean water, healthy food and our neighbors to exist. In the end, you won't be able to drink that $50 bill. And yet, the change is a process that takes time and planning. Just like planning for retirement, you can plan, step by step, to remove yourself from the gridlock of corporate life and learn to create self-sufficient communities. Community gardens, hunting clubs, shared wells, bartering, smaller community power supplies and other innovative community designs could go a long way to disconnect you from feeding the corporate interests.

Every decision we make determines where we put our resources, as well as how we get our needs met. What can you replace in your life that will end your own dependence on the corporate power? Will you begin to wean yourself from Wal-Mart and other stores that stock slave-made merchandise from China and Southeast Asia sweatshops?

What sustainable alternatives could we find to replace the need to clear-cut the forests to make toilet paper? How much is your diet and lifestyle affecting your relationship to medication and health care? Do you feed off McDonald's then look to the corporations who control the health care industry to heal you? How can you wean yourself from doctors through adjusting your own habits and self-care?

What if the market crashed and food that you now buy from box supermarkets shipped in from California was gone? What if you had to survive off the land? Could you? Being willing to consider the worst-case scenario is a way to be prepared. If you never consider the potential, how can you be prepared to face it, if and when it arrives?

No Action is Too Small

On a local and more immediate level, every small act becomes a part of many small acts on the part of many individuals that add up to a larger action, which then becomes a movement. Part of your challenge is finding your rightful place within the movement. What action can you take, today, to stand up for justice and Democracy?

Not everyone can protest. Getting arrested in an act of civil disobedience is not an option for everyone. But you can:

- ✓ Educate yourself and encourage others to educate themselves
- ✓ Develop critical thinking
- ✓ Watch wiseye.com and see what is really taking place in our government, while it is happening
- ✓ Write letters to your representatives demanding election reform
- ✓ Volunteer to work with organizations that align with your personal mission: League of Conservation Voters, ACLU, Planned Parenthood or other local or state groups helping to support Democracy
- ✓ Contribute food to shelters and food banks to help take up the slack from elimination of services for low-income and poor families
- ✓ Move information via blogs and Facebook accounts
- ✓ Walk a picket line
- ✓ Volunteer to watch your votes being counted
- ✓ Talk to and educate your clerk on the dangers of voting machines
- ✓ Become a poll worker
- ✓ Run for office
- ✓ Attend Senate and Assembly meetings and observe your government in action
- ✓ Get people registered to vote
- ✓ Work with Move To Amend (groups of citizens committed to overturning Citizens United, the ruling that established corporations as "people")
- ✓ Go to your city and county board meetings
- ✓ Communicate with your representatives

There are opportunities everywhere for you to make a difference and contribute needed resources to build the coalition of reform. But only you can make the decision to act.

"Legislation," Wisconsin State Capitol

ELECTION PROTECTION: HAND COUNT PAPER BALLOTS

Perhaps the most rudimentary issue before us is the protection of our elections. I encourage everyone to take action to move forward the reform of how votes are counted. We must overturn laws that disenfranchise voters and protect the voting machine vendors, and create new systems to accommodate observable hand count paper ballot elections for the path to election reform to take hold.

Like Wisconsin's peace and justice movement, the Election Integrity movement has been a part of the infrastructure of the United States for over a decade. Since Jim Collier and his brother Kenneth wrote their ground-breaking book, *Votescam,* election fraud has grown to international proportions. But vigilant journalists like Brad Friedman, Bob Fitrakis and Bev Harris have been working for years documenting the truth about this mafia-type industry. The manufacture and sale of voting machines that can flip votes has appeared to slowly but surely turn the entire country into neoconservatives. The message is, "Pay no attention to the man behind the curtain, because there isn't one."

Get Involved With Election Reform

Standing up for fair and open elections has the same emotional challenges as standing up for Democracy in the middle of a corporate takeover of the government. The thought of rigged elections can bring a hopelessness that leads to people not voting. What's the use, they might say, if our votes are being stolen?

As difficult as it is to face the shock and awe of this, we simply must. And we can. Part of the reform will come from facing the potential hopelessness of the situation and finding a way to effectively channel it into nonviolent action of reform. Hope comes from within, and part of finding hope is facing facts so you can be prepared. But instead of using fear and rage to get even, turn them into passion and let them inspire you to take action.

The following is an excerpt from a paper written by Sheila Parks, PhD and Founder of Center for Hand-Counted Paper Ballots, and Grant W. Petty, Professor of Atmospheric Science at University of Wisconsin-Madison after the Supreme Court recount in May 2011:

> *Election fraud is not just a hypothetical concern. In addition to strong circumstantial evidence in countless other cases, instances of clear fraud have been uncovered that led to actual indictments in Cuyahoga County, Ohio, and Clay County, Kentucky. Echoes of Cuyahoga can be heard (by those inclined to hear them) in the recent Waukesha recount.*
>
> *Experts on election integrity have been sounding two main alarms for at least ten years: (1) it's far too easy to rig elections in ways that are difficult to detect, and (2) there is considerable circumstantial evidence that it is regularly occurring.*
>
> *Consider this: Approximately 1.48 million votes were cast in the Prosser v. Kloppenburg election. The final published difference between them was a mere 7,004 votes, so flipping only 3,502 of them could have given the election back to Kloppenburg. That's only a single vote flipped (or, alternatively, two Prosser votes simply discarded) per 422 cast!*
>
> *Now consider this: Electronic voting machines use proprietary software to tabulate votes. Not even election officials are allowed to view or test the integrity of the*

software or the memory cards. The counting of votes simply cannot be observed or verified by the voting public or the election officials. It is impossible to know whether it is being done correctly and honestly. We are being told to take it on faith that the voting machine vendors, and those who have access to the machines, are honest. This is not merely risky, it is fundamentally antithetical to Democracy.

The Emmy-nominated documentary Hacking Democracy (free viewing online, 81 min.) presents a shocking demonstration of how easily electronic votes can be hacked, and it also offers troubling evidence that election rigging is actually occurring. Even if you don't read beyond this point, please view Hacking Democracy and urge family, friends, and acquaintances to watch it as well. You will never view our elections or electronic voting machines the same way again.

We're accustomed to hearing the phrase "innocent until proven guilty" applied to suspects being tried for crimes, and that's as it should be. But we in the United States, more so than in many other developed countries, inappropriately apply the same standard of evidence to our elections. Our naive assumption is that unless unambiguous evidence of fraud or gross error is actually uncovered, it most likely didn't occur. If you can't see it, it must not exist. This is what those who corrupt the election process count on.

Election fraud, like any crime, requires both motive and opportunity. And ample motive can already be found on either side of the current ideological divide in our country.

Imagine the zealous conservative who sincerely believes that abortion is murder and that liberal politicians are therefore condoning murder on a large scale. Or imagine the zealous liberal who sincerely believes that conservative policies will condemn the earth to perish, and soon, from runaway greenhouse warming. Either of these individuals might be persuaded that it's morally justified and urgently necessary to commit election fraud in defense of humankind.

Would anyone who cares about honest elections deliberately put either person in charge of actually overseeing and enforcing election procedures? But that's exactly what we do with our partisan elections for county clerks!

As we saw in the last recount, many judgment calls were made as to which ballots would be declared valid and which discarded. And whenever judgment is in play, so is bias. If you are unfortunate enough to live in a county or municipality where your election officials oppose the party or candidate you support, you should be very, very concerned about whether your vote will be fairly counted.

But it doesn't stop at the county level. Consider further the wealthy industrialist who quite plausibly believes that if a certain pro-regulation candidate for Congress loses, s/he and their allies stand to make millions of dollars more per year. Might s/he not be tempted to invest considerable political and financial capital in getting voting machines adopted that can be easily and undetectably hacked? Would they perhaps even get into the business of building them?

We may never be able to eliminate the motive, but we can, and we must, identify and eliminate the opportunities to undetectably rig our elections. Until we do, we cannot rationally assume that elections are clean and fair. And we therefore cannot rationally trust the official outcomes of elections.

Here, in summary, are the major weak links in Wisconsin elections:

Vote tabulation. Can we be certain votes are being honestly and correctly tabulated by electronic devices? No. Unfortunately, current procedures and the electronic voting machines themselves provide absolutely no way to independently verify the accuracy of electronic vote counts short of a full hand recount of paper ballots. And by Wisconsin law, most of the recount must be done on the same electronic voting machines that could have been hacked in the first place. Be aware that the memory and printouts can be made to differ from the real voter intent and that the pre-election testing is useless for detecting fraudulent programming!

Also, although required by Wisconsin law, touchscreen machines used in some districts were found to provide no paper record and thus no voter-verifiable (or recountable) record of the vote!

Chain of custody. For the purposes of a recount, are we ensuring that ballots can't be added or subtracted between the time they are cast by the voter and the time they are recounted? As we clearly saw in the recent Wisconsin Supreme Court recount, the mandated procedures for our elections are not always followed. Citizen observers witnessed a stunning range of abnormalities in the labeling/sealing of ballot bags and even discovered a poll tape dated March 30, days before the election. The poll tape in question, with its time stamp of 1:40 AM, was sworn to as actual votes. This claim was later retracted only when persistently questioned.

[In the May recount, we] sampled just some of the evidence suggesting that the upcoming [Summer] recall elections in Wisconsin cannot, and should not, simply be trusted to be honest. Now we come to the most important part: What can still be done to restore confidence in the outcomes?

Contact your county and municipal clerks, the election inspectors and the mayor and councilpersons or the town chair and the supervisors. They can authorize the little extra money that it would take to hand-count paper ballots (HCPB) for [elections] in your municipality. Talk to them about the many jurisdictions in Wisconsin and elsewhere that already count their ballots by hand. Acton, Maine (with seven races and two initiatives, six teams of two people each—a Republican and a Democrat—were able to hand-count, twice, 944 ballots in four hours) and Lyndeborough, New Hampshire are potential models for the rest of the country.

Volunteer to serve in non-partisan citizen exit polls being organized by the Election Defense Alliance to rigorously and independently verify vote tabulations and chain-of-custody of ballots.

Our final prediction: Unless the Wisconsin recalls are hand-counted in every race, with secure hand-counted paper ballots (HCPB) elections, at least some of them will be rigged, with major implications for the balance of power in the Statehouse.

Alarmist? Perhaps. But the only way to be certain is to act immediately to close the massive security holes in our elections. Please use social media to share the information and links in this article, and help educate those who naively think that outcome of the recall elections depends solely on getting out the vote, who votes and how they vote.

Protecting election integrity is not 'left' or 'right.' If any commentator or political leader actively objects to making our elections more secure, please ask yourself what their real stake is in the current deeply flawed system.

There are many steps you can take to become a part of election reform:

Begin with your own education. Read election integrity journalists like Brad Friedman, Bev Harris and Bob Fitrakis.

Join an Election Integrity Group Join Wisconsin Citizens for Election Protection, Wisconsin Counts, Election Defense Alliance Wisconsin, or any other group working to protect elections. Find a small group of concerned citizens in your town and work together with your city council, county board and legislators to lobby for hand count paper ballots and election reforms.

Learn the truth about Wisconsin election laws. Did you know a Wisconsin county clerk can be charged with a felony if, after the machine tallies the votes after the polls close, she decided to hand count them, just to double check? Learn the function of the Government Accountability Board,[93] and write them as well as your legislators to demand hand count paper ballots.

Get to know your clerks. Educate them on the need for hand count paper ballots. Before the next election, make an appointment and go talk to them. Tell them you would like to exercise your right as a US citizen to observe the polls after they close, and watch your votes being counted. Make sure they are offering paper ballots, and urge them not to encourage people to use the touchscreen machines.

Refuse to Vote on Touchscreens. Call ahead and make sure your clerk knows why you refuse to use the machines,

---

93 http://gab.wi.gov/elections-voting

and tell them to make sure to provide paper ballots on election day.

Write-in Your Vote. Even if your candidate is on the ballot, if you write-in their name in the write-in option, along with their party, the machine will force the ballot into a separate bin for hand-counting after the polls close. In this way you can make sure your vote is hand counted.

File an Open Records Request. A little known action that you can take immediately after the election is to file an Open Records Request with your ward to see all the ballots cast, and then gather a team to hand count them yourselves. This request must be done before they destroy the ballots and is your right as a citizen.

We need voices being raised all over the state from citizens who understand the urgency of this needed reform. When they steal our votes, they steal our voices, and then they steal our power. With our stolen votes, they can place any person they wish into the place of power delegated to public servants, and they can, in turn, implement any bill into law that their sponsors wish, regardless of how the people feel. The 2011 Assembly Republicans all pledged allegiance to Jeff Fitzgerald, who in turn ushered through ALEC bills at an alarming rate.

Over and over, as the Walker administration demonstrates its allegiance to corporations, more and more people rise up and demand justice. But how do you talk about election protection without sounding like a "tin hat conspiracy theorist?" How can you inspire your family, friends and neighbors to learn for themselves that this is really happening, when they are addicted to corporate media messages and incapable of critical thinking?

Transformation will take place when citizens stop listening only to mainstream media and start researching beyond what the Milwaukee Journal Sentinel or the NY Times prints. Social media like Twitter and Facebook are the new raw truth. Information flows from so many sources, and first-hand reports will give a much more accurate picture of what's happening. Uncensored and uncut, WCMC, Facebook, Twitter and other social media websites are where you should seek the news and then decide for yourself.

But more important, observe your government in action. Participation in the election systems by the people demanding change is what will save Wisconsin right now. Our voices raised louder and longer with the truth is allowing the truth to be heard. More and more people know more and more of what is truly taking place. Tides are turning because We the People are speaking up, even if it seems hopeless.

Nothing should stop you from raising your voice: it is your duty. If you sit by and do nothing, they will steal your vote and use it against us. That is why I *tell* you, don't *ask* you: take action today to help protect our elections.

Wisconsin's Story
Wisconsin represents a microcosm of the whole. We have evidence of judicial, media, legislative and election fraud, involving corrupt people, hackable voting machines, and laws passed over ten years time that have left us unprotected.

Research election fraud in this country, ALEC, media fraud and the justice systems. Understand how they are all working together to destroy our government. Once you put the picture together, sit down for a moment and take a deep breath. Let yourself scream and cry and rage that this is truly what has happened to this country. Process the *shock and awe* involved in realizing you have been lied to, and that those lies may have misguided you to assist in our own destruction. Whether you voted for Republicans or Tea Party candidates because you believed their lies, or you ignored the truth because you felt powerless against it, allow yourself an understandable emotional reaction so you can reconnect again with your feelings.

Only instead of seeking revenge on the traitors, help change the system at its root. Our mantra? Repeat this, over and over, at every turn, in every meeting, in line at the supermarket and during commercials at Packer games: Observable hand count paper ballot elections. **Demand** open and transparent elections.

We the People of the United States of America, in order to form a more perfect union ... demand open, transparent and fair elections, and honest and accurate voting systems. Demand the removal of all machines that come between us and our votes. Nothing short of hand count paper ballots being observed by all will do.

What will it take to get you to take action now?

Resources

Victoria Collier, Votescam.org
Victoria Collier is a seasoned activist, organizer, writer and editor, with over 20 years of experience in the non-profit sector. Daughter and niece of James and Kenneth Collier, investigative journalists and authors of the ground-breaking book *Votescam: The Stealing of America*. After the death of her father in 1998, Victoria continued to speak and write on the threat to Democracy posed by computerized voting machines, appearing on radio shows nationwide, and as a special guest lecturer and panel member at the Institute for Policy Studies in Washington D.C. She has continued to update the Votescam investigation into computerized vote fraud, and the book's current printing contains her own writing and reporting. The book has become a motivating force and how-to manual for anyone seeking to truly reform our election system.
https://www.facebook.com/victoria.collier3
contact@votescam.org

Brad Friedman, Bradblog.com
The publisher and Executive Editor of The BRAD BLOG is also an L.A.-based investigative journalist/blogger, political commentator, broadcaster, author, Commonwealth Institute Fellow. Brad's extensive work in election integrity reaching back 20 years makes his library an invaluable investigation on all facets of election fraud being perpetrated in this country.
http://www.Bradblog.com
7095 Hollywood Blvd., #594
Los Angeles, CA 90028
brad@bradblog.com

Bob Fitrakis, Free Press
This professor/author/journalist/media host literally wrote the book on US election fraud. He has authored, co-authored, collaborated or contributed to most of the major election fraud investigation, including *How the GOP Stole America's 2004 Election & Is Rigging 2008*, written with Harvey Wasserman. Currently a Green Party candidate for Senate in Ohio District 3.
http://freepress.org/columns/display/3
1021 E. Broad St
Columbus, OH 43205
614.253.2571
truth@freepress.org

Election Protection
The nonpartisan Election Protection coalition was formed to ensure that all voters have an equal opportunity to participate in the political process. Through their state of the art hotlines: 1-866-OUR-VOTE (administered by the Lawyers' Committee for Civil Rights Under Law) and 1-888-Ve-Y-Vota (administered by the National Association of Latino Elected and Appointed Officials Education Fund), their website, and comprehensive voter protection field programs across the country, they provide Americans from coast to coast with comprehensive voter information and advice on how they can make sure their vote is counted.
http://www.866ourvote.org/

Bev Harris, Black Box Voting
Harris has been on the trail of election fraud since before her documentary, *Black Box Voting* was released in 2008. Author and investigative journalist, her current exposé involves the purging of thousands of voters from the rolls. A tireless advocate for reforming all areas of US elections, Harris has created a website for citizens to report their findings and keep up on the latest news in election integrity.
http://blackboxvoting.org/
crew@blackboxvoting.org
330 SW 43rd St. Suite K
PMB 547
Renton WA 98057
206.335.7747

Sheila Parks, Center for Hand Count Paper Ballots
Long-time human rights activist, former teacher, professor, and media host, Parks has focused on studying US voting systems since the 2000 presidential election. Her Center for Hand Count Paper Ballots advocates for removal of voting machines and creating transparent and fair HCPB elections.
http://www.handcountedpaperballots.org
info@handcountedpaperballots.org
Center for Hand-Counted Paper Ballots
617.744.6020

Verified Voting
Lists of all states in the USA and the kind of election equipment used in 2010 in all the jurisdictions in each state.
http://verifiedvoting.org/

Complaint to the US Department of Justice

August 16, 2011

TO: Bruce Gear
Department of Justice
bruce.gear@usdofj.gov

FROM: Barbara With

RE: Election Fraud in Wisconsin

Dear Mr. Gear:

Thank you so much for taking my call last week and inviting me to submit my complaint about Wisconsin election fraud to the Department of Justice.

In the past, election fraud has been notoriously difficult to prove. Aside from the untraceable corruption of the voting machine software, those using election fraud to gain political power have gone on to change statutes that make it exceeding more difficult to prosecute. However, the scope of fraud that Wisconsin is experiencing stretches beyond just election systems. One must akin the entirety of the election, judicial, legislative, and media fraud with which we are being assaulted to a nonviolent war: all levels of our culture are under attack—economic, educational, environmental, community, political—as those perpetrating election fraud infiltrate our State with the intent to instigate a hostile takeover of our government.

Judicial fraud ranges from the Supreme Court, who allowed Citizens United to become a law, to David Prosser, the Wisconsin judge under investigation for assaulting a fellow judge, and whose seat on the bench we believe was rigged for him.

Legislative fraud can be found in the Koch-funded American Legislative Exchange Commission, a right wing center that inspired all the fraudulent legislation the Republicans introduced into the State in January.

Media fraud includes Rupurt Murdoch, currently under investigation for his illegal activity, and his station "Fox News," who have purposefully and with intent generated false representation of events taking place within the State, and consistently provide the Republicans a platform to broadcast lies, deception and fraud touted as "news."

Waging this nonviolent war against the citizens of this state and nation amounts to treason. As those engaging in fraudulent activity use their power to enact laws that directly undermine the US and

Wisconsin Constitution, they provide direct proof that they are traitors. No metal detector at the airport will protect me from this kind of terrorism.

To this end, my complaint will address specifically the election fraud we are currently experiencing in Wisconsin, but I respectfully ask that you consider passing this on to someone who is RICO compliant.

Racketeer Influenced and Corrupt Organizations Act

From my limited understanding, RICO provides for extended criminal penalties and a civil cause of action for acts performed as part of an ongoing criminal organization. The RICO Act focuses specifically on racketeering and allows for the leaders of a syndicate to be tried for the crimes that they ordered others to do.

I also understand there must be one of four specified relationships between the defendants and the enterprise present:

1) the defendants invested the proceeds of the pattern of racketeering activity into the enterprise;

2) the defendants acquired or maintained an interest in, or control over, the enterprise through the pattern of racketeering activity;

3) the defendants conducted or participated in the affairs of the enterprise "through" the pattern of racketeering activity; or

4) the defendants conspired to do one of the above. I believe Wisconsin has been hit with all four.

I am requesting the Department of Justice to investigate Wisconsin as the enterprise, that is now a victim of the Defendants, including but not limited to Karl Rove, George Bush and the Republican Party; the Wisconsin Republican Party; Kevin Kennedy and the Wisconsin Government Accountability Board; Dominion, Sequoia, ES&S, Command Central, et al voting machine and systems distributors and manufacturers; David H. and Charles G. Koch, Koch Industries, Inc., Americans For Prosperity and the Tea Party; and Chris Cline and The Cline Group to name a few. These Defendants collectively acquired or maintained an interest in, or control over, "the enterprise" (Wisconsin) through the pattern of racketeering activity, namely, the use of fraudulent voting systems to gain legislative control to rewrite and enact legislation to benefit the defendants and bankrupt the State in order to declare financial martial law to seize our land, natural resources, monetary funds, and to control industry, government, banking and law enforcement in a hostile takeover.

I also respectfully ask that you investigate the possibility that the defendants are "investing the proceeds of the pattern of racketeering activity into the enterprise" by planning to use Wisconsin resources and laborers to produce the fraudulent voting machines to sell around the world, which then includes selling the ability for any country to control their elections.

Because of the scope of this complaint, in order to present this case to RICO, I have included facts and sources beyond Wisconsin to demonstrate what I believe is a repeated pattern of illegal action over the past decade on a national level. I have also provided references for people who you can contact for further evidence in each area of fraud who will be more than happy to help with an investigation.

Recovering from this sweeping election, judicial, legislative, and media fraud will be challenging. But if we don't act quickly, we may never recover from the environmental damage being done to the State and the country. Fraudulent politicians are allowing out-of-state mining companies to control the legislation governing mining laws. Currently, companies are setting up sand frac mines in Chippewa County at lighting speed, the largest one being 234 acres. Enormous health risks threaten the lives of all citizens of the state, as well as the ground water, land and air. The "jobs" claimed to be created are actually temp workers hired from Manpower for low wages, with no benefits, no health insurance, no vacation pay, and six to seven day work weeks. This activity proves that these criminals have no regard for the true health and wellbeing of our state.

With the support of Wisconsin Republicans, the mining corporations are being allowed to disregard the environment, lie to local officials and the public about the jobs and the risks, conceal crucial facts concerning the industry's horrific record of verifiable toxic pollution, and ignore the truth of the environmental warfare being waged in other parts of the country, such as Yellowstone, and the Gulf of Mexico (where the corporations hold the clean-up hostage by demanding taxpayers pay for their mistakes by threatening the government with more pollution or inaction). Add the speed at which the mines are going up, and we are mortified of the potentially terrifying environmental disaster being created daily.

In northern Wisconsin, we are currently fighting Cline Mine and its intention to blow up 20 miles of the Penokee Mountains in the Upper Peninsula, thereby threatening to destroy the Bad River Band, the biggest employer in the area, who has already issued a resolution opposing it and has gathered a powerful legal team to stand against it. Their autocratic actions are threatening to destroy not only our communities and way of life, but also the water, air and land quality. Cline, with its proven record of disastrous mining projects that have left areas devastated with toxic waste, has been lying to the public and county officials for months about their intention and past records of pollution around the world.

That the mining companies are being allowed to write the mining legislation is the biggest fraud of all.

I will also ask you to investigate Senator Ron Johnson's ties to this collusion. Out of nowhere, he came unknown onto the scene with no political experience and defeated a beloved Wisconsin progressive voice of reason, Russ Feingold. If you asked yourself, what if the vote was stolen, now Johnson brings nepotism into his ties to mining and plastics, via his father-in-law. In fact, I would like an investigation into Johnson to see if he really was a part of the

Pacur Company before the plan to put him into office began, and what the $10 million dollar kickback he just received from Pacur is about. Last I heard he still had not produced the documents confirming that was a "bonus." Some believe he was placed there by his father-in-law who also does business with Rio Tinto Mines out of Australia, who own Kennicutt Mines in Utah, who have ties to Wisconsin mines in Flambeau.

Also include a look into how Johnson et al will profit from plastic. If Cline Mine continues to pollute in Wisconsin as it has worldwide, our water will soon be undrinkable, and water-bottling plants will need to go into high gear. Water is the new gold, and plastics are used in making voting machines.

Then please continue by investigating Rich Zipperer (R) and Mark Honadel (R) who are sponsored by the mining companies. They appear to be working in collusion with national Republicans to strip protection from the Great Lakes Pact. At a recent hearing they presented their plan to divert water from Lake Michigan. Could they be preparing to up the sales of bottled water? More profit for Pacur. They are also supporting secrecy of how much water Cline Mine thinks they will use from Lake Superior. None of this bodes well for the people of the State, and we have a witness who will attest that the minutes of a recent hearing revealed that they had changed her testimony to wrongly reflect support, when she clearly expressed dissent. How much is this happening with these fraudulent politicians in power?

And lastly, please investigate if these corporations plan to begin manufacturing the fraudulent voting machines in Wisconsin. What would be needed? Plastics and silver among other things. All the players are in place: Koch buying the elections via fraud—voter suppression, vote flipping, corrupt officials, illegal and misleading mailers, and selling corrupt voting machines worldwide; Johnson, Ryan, and Duffy working to undo protections on the national level; Walker's mining and trucking friends and cronies all gaining while Wisconsin's coffers are being emptied, our rights are being stripped including freedom of speech, freedom of assembly and the right to collective bargain; our resources are being exploited and polluted; our communities are being purposefully starved; our elderly and disabled are being cut off from support; our water is being threatened; and I believe, we are on the verge of martial law. This truly is a war.

Please investigate the bigger plan, that the Defendants created a political party, the Tea Party, and are using the fraudulent media to fuel dissent among the people, breed hatred and fear, broadcast propaganda, and incite citizens to blame the current administration thereby removing the focus from the Defendants. The insidious part is that the Defendants did not even need their votes. They just needed the large numbers to make it look like all the votes they were about to steal were legitimate. This gave the appearance that The People have moved to the neo-conservative right and the

Defendants can continue to fund the industrial war complex. In 2008, we know now $16 trillion dollars of our federal money was handed over to the banking industry. So they raided our coffers, devalued our property and credit rating, bankrupted our cities, and now have the power to pollute our land, water and air, and claim on their fraudulent media stations that it's the unions and teachers' pensions.

Today, August 16, Wisconsin has two more recall elections. Election protection groups around the world will be analyzing and documenting the patterns that have been played out across America for years without recourse. Each time they fit the pattern that proves fraud, it's too late, as another election is stolen, another truth suppressed, another lie told, and another illegal piece of legislation passed to close our Democracy and destroy the citizens of this state and this country.

So if the recall election votes flip tonight for Kim Simac in Jim Holperin's district, the entire world will see in action this fraudulent machine I want you to investigate. At one time, the Tea Party might have been able to inspire people to vote for them, though we can never know, since our election system is so corrupt. Tonight, it will be their undoing. I believe the last Tea Party rally in Wisconsin netted about ten people. The easiest exit poll I know. Simac wins, and Mr. Gear, I think your investigation should begin immediately.

With more and more of the masses understanding election, legislative, judicial and media fraud, more and more Americans will be standing up to demand what I am demanding: investigation into this RICO situation

There is no lack of evidence of fraud in Wisconsin: we ARE the evidence. There is however, a lack of accountability running rampant through this country to prosecute it. No branch of government is immune to corruption. Even the Department of Justice is not immune. So I ask, Mr. Gear, where do the good citizens of Wisconsin go to for help at this late date? We need heroes in every level of government to stand up for Democracy and take action to protect our votes.

Mr. Gear, will you be one of the heroes who acts to help restore justice to Wisconsin and the nation? Or will you be another tool in the takeover?

Please, won't you stand up for Democracy and help us restore justice to the state of Wisconsin. From here, we will go on to help reform the nation. Our very lives and the life of the Republic depend on it.

Urgently,
Barbara With

COMPLAINT
[To better understand the scope of my complaint, please reference Attachment One: A History and Proof of Election Fraud, Legislative, Judicial and Media Fraud in Regards to Stealing Elections.]

I believe Wisconsin is the enterprise, and has been the victim of the following Defendants, including but not limited to Karl Rove, George Bush and the Republican Party; the Wisconsin Republican Party including but not limited to Scott Walker, Scott Fitzgerald, Jeff Fitzgerald, Alberta Darling, Robin Vos, Ron Johnson, Paul Ryan, Sean Duffy, et al; Kevin Kennedy and the Wisconsin Government Accountability Board; Dominion, Sequoia, ES&S, Command Central, et al voting machine and systems distributors and manufacturers; David H. and Charles G. Koch, Koch Industries, Inc., Americans For Prosperity and the Tea Party; Chris Cline and The Cline Group; Fox News, Glenn Beck, Russ Limbaugh, and Vicki McKenna at al news media propagandists, to name a few. These defendants collectively acquired or maintained an interest in, or control over, "the enterprise" (Wisconsin) through the pattern of racketeering activity, namely, the use of fraudulent voting systems to gain legislative control to rewrite and enact legislation to benefit the Defendants and bankrupt the State in order to declare financial martial law to seize our land, natural resources, monetary funds, and to control industry, government, banking and law enforcement in a hostile takeover

Wisconsin Election Fraud: Supreme Court Recount
In May 2011, I was an observer at the Wisconsin Supreme Court recount of the Kloppenburg-Prosser contest. In that election, Joanne Kloppenburg was declared the winner, until two days later when Waukesha County Clerk Kathy Nickolaus, a former assistant to Prosser, "found" 14,000 votes that flipped the election to Prosser. Because the total difference fell within the requirement, Kloppenburg was afforded a state-sponsored recount. At that time Congresswoman Tammy Baldwin (D-WI) also asked the Department of Justice to open an investigation.
http://www.forbes.com/sites/rickungar/2011/04/13/something-smells-in-waukesha-county-wisconsin-and-its-not-the-cheese/

As one of the observers for Kloppenburg, I spent a week at Franklin and Waukesha. I and other very concerned citizens were uncovering what turned out to be a steady stream of shocking anomalies. Over 800 incidents, including but not limited to no seal numbers; crossed off seal numbers; bags that had been slit and ducked tape shut; ballot bags with gaping holes big enough to get ballots in and out; poll tape votes from an Eagle Touchscreen voting machine dated March 30, 2011 1:40 AM; and bag numbers crossed off and re-written that did not match the seal numbers. We gathered over 2000 photographs of the evidence and presented them to the Kloppenburg campaign as well as informing the Government Accountability Board.

http://www.bradblog.com/?p=8531

What we found should have instigated an immediate investigation. Instead, the Wisconsin Government Accountability Board headed by Kevin Kennedy quickly declared Prosser the winner. We were appalled, not just that the blatant and frightening number of anomalies were overlooked, but that Prosser was quickly waved onto the bench in time to overturn, in record time, Judge Sumi's ruling in March that the Republicans broke the law, again, by violating our open meeting laws.

This has, in turn, allowed the Republicans to continue breaking the law by using their power to pass illegal "laws" that are denying us our US and Wisconsin Constitutional rights and threatening the very existence of the state. (See Attachment Two: Illegal Activities, Legislative Fraud and Collusion on the part of Wisconsin Republicans).

Filing a Complaint with the GAB

On June 10, 2011, I filed a formal complaint with the GAB, demanding an investigation into Kathy Nickolaus and GAB Director Kevin Kennedy for their part in not only declaring Prosser the winner in the face of the evidence, but for bringing the fraudulent voting machines and voter registration systems into the state.
https://docs.google.com/document/d/1NR7EuRDoQu9pXu5k1d7m5pOeP4K-6zmnRSRtA-xdFg4/edit?hl=en_US

Wisconsin Citizens for Election Protection

Because of the demonstrated corruption taking place and the lack of oversight on the part of our GAB, citizen observers from the recount formed Wisconsin Citizens for Election Protection (WCEP), as well as joining forces with Election Defense Alliance, a national election protection organization that pulls together grass roots Election Integrity people from around the country. Together, we have been working diligently to put safeguards in place to protect our recall elections since our GAB will not. Lead by two former clerks, WCEP began a full-out campaign to work with county clerks, the GAB and citizens. Hundreds of Wisconsin citizens across the state stepped up and were trained to observe after the polls closed. We also organized and conducted exit polls at several of the key polling places where we suspected fraud might be perpetrated. In addition, we called in experts in all areas of election fraud, including Brad Friedman, Bev Harris, Sheila Parks, Jeannie Dean, Sally Castleman, Jonathan Simon, and Richard Charnin, election statistics analyst, and conducted studies on not only the results of the Supreme Court recount, but the now the recall elections of August 9 and August 16.
www.electionprotectionwisconsin.com

House Committee On Election Reform June 9, 2011

On June 9, 2011 I testified before the Wisconsin Assembly Committee for Election Reform. At this meeting, Rep. Pridemore, the Republican co-sponsoring the new bill to bring in voting machines with permanent software, admitted he knew how to flip voting machines, but tried to assure me the "new machines were safe." Unfortunately, no voting machines can ever be safe as long as the vote counting takes place in secrecy on machines proven to be fraudulent and owned by corporations with known ties to

the Defendants. Hear my testimony, stating that the only solution is to restore hand count paper ballots with open and transparent systems. (My testimony begins at about 2:06)
http://www.wiseye.org/Programming/VideoArchive/EventDetail.aspx?evhdid=4358

Election Fraud Continues

All throughout the recall process, the Republicans, Tea Party and Americans For Prosperity have been committing election fraud without consequence. Complaints were made to the GAB but little or no action has been taken. (See Attachment Three: *Election Fraud Activities on the Part of the Republicans, Tea Party, Americans For Prosperity of Wisconsin et al.)*

GAB Board Meeting, August 2, 2011

Because of our enormous concern for the safety of our recall elections, members of the WCEP and other patriotic citizens testified at the GAB Board meeting August 2, 2011. As you will see in this video, Director Kevin Kennedy attempts to discredit us by referring to us as "conspiracy theorists" and instead of addressing our real concern about our elections bring stolen, disputes our evidence and testimony and once again defends the voting machine companies. It was also apparent at this meeting that the actual judges on the Board may not be receiving all information, and certainly Judge Barland appeared to be startled at hearing all of us plead for measures to be put in place.
http://www.wiseye.org/Programming/VideoArchive/EventDetail.aspx?evhdid=4522

After the meeting, I e-mailed Kevin Kennedy asking if my complaint regarding Kathy Nickolaus and him ever made it to the Board members. The response I received from Kennedy and ethics director Becker confirm that they censor what the actual Board hears and see and, no, in fact, they did not pass the complaint on to the Board. Further correspondence reveals Kennedy actually has no real oversight, since his "bosses" the GAB only see what he allows them and in order to complain to them, you have to get through the staff censors.
https://docs.google.com/document/d/1mAmzXG5nHp97nYUlVpGySnbdfRZq_7eFOBU9F5o03CU/edit?hl=en_US

Back in 2005, Kennedy, despite warnings from his staff, politicians, election integrity activists around the country, repeated protests and even a lawsuit filed to stop him, unilaterally took it upon himself to enter into a contract with Accenture, formerly Arthur Andersen, fraudulent accountants for ENRON, to handle our voter registration system. This decision demonstrated that Kennedy has knowingly and intentionally put my vote at risk.
https://docs.google.com/document/d/1L4st5t_wVovvJHAo-9ze7NovrRAo2fxnDsyqOOTaq34/edit?hl=en_US

I am asking the Department of Justice to investigate this fraud at the GAB, as well as the Republican and Tea Parties of Wisconsin, and to help us gain back control of our state by supporting our movement to reform how elections take place. We want hand count paper ballots, as well as reforming the statues to protect the citizens and our votes, not the staff and corporations.

We have years of ample evidence by reputed universities, testimony and documentation by the people who actually program the software, and a national Election Protection movement that has been more stealthy than Homeland Security in monitoring, documenting and reporting on the repetitive patterns of vote-stealing that has taken place in the country over the past decade that shows the repeated fraudulent activity perpetrated by the Defendants.

America has been lied to and lulled to sleep by media fraud of the propaganda machine that is working over time. We do not lack evidence; we lack accountable patriots like our Wisconsin Democrats who, when they saw the truth coming down the tracks—the well-orchestrated takeover of our government—left the State to give the citizens time to learn the truth: Wisconsin, as well as Michigan, Ohio, Indiana, Arizona, Florida and now Minnesota are coming under attack because we have access to the last great fresh water bodies in the world and rich wilderness of untouched minerals, and now criminals in power waging this nonviolent war against us.

The results of last week's recall election were as troubling as we expected. Our exit polls are way off the results and once again Waukesha County, and Kathy Nickolaus, a woman currently under investigation for election fraud at the Supreme Court recount, was in charge of one of the key spots the Republicans needed to keep SD8. Monitoring of the results ward by ward show the same patterns of flipping as have played out, and a murky trail of questions that we demand to be answered.

ATTACHMENT ONE

A Definition, History and Proof of Election, Legislative, Judicial and Media Fraud in Regards to Stealing Elections

Definition of Election Fraud

Election fraud is not just corrupted officials;

- It's not just voting machines that can be rigged with no discernible trace and proven by Princeton and other universities;
- It's not just gerrymandering by redistricting using $395 an hour attorneys at taxpayer cost to draw up secret maps;
- It's not just a voter suppression law that outright keeps voters from the polls and was rammed through the legislature;
- It's not just confusion on Election Day by closing polling places, not informing the public, and providing clerks with confusing information;
- It's not just threatening to close DMVs in Democratic districts where IDs can be obtained;
- It's not just Americans for Prosperity sending out Absentee Ballot Application forms to Democrats with erroneous information;
- It's not just propaganda that makes people believe the state has turned red to "balance the budget";
- It's not just a right-wing "ALEC"-type organization named "Election Center" the brainchild of the voting machine companies and now a staple for election officials who support the corruptible voting machines;
- It's not just a Government "Accountability" Board whose staff censors information getting to Board Members for the express purpose of tampering with elections.

It's all this and more and Wisconsin has verifiable PROOF that election fraud is alive and functioning well in this State.

****

History of and Proof of Election Fraud

The case for election fraud in the United States is made by the Justice Integrity Project ("The Project"), a research and education initiative established in 2010 by concerned citizens to improve oversight of abusive prosecutorial and judicial decisions in the federal justice system. In this article are all the contact names and documentation through the past ten years of election fraud in the US.
http://justice-integrity.org/index.php?option=com_content&view=article&id=453%3Acutting-through-vote-fraud-claims-hypocrisy&catid=44%3Amyblog

This expose done by Dan Rather in 2007 should serve as ample evidence of fraud on the part of the voting machine companies.
http://www.bradblog.com/?p=4960

Scientists at Princeton Hack a Voting Machine:
http://www.liveleak.com/view?i=a8d_1194275446

Perhaps the most trouble piece of the election fraud puzzle is how the government passed HAVA, the ***Help America Vote Act.*** And voting machines, manufactured by Diebold with strong ties to Rove, Bush, and the Republican Party, not only became mandatory, but the US government provided millions of dollars to bring them into polling places across America. At the same time, an organization called the *Election Center* was started, touted as a nonpartisan organization, but voting machine companies provided start-up funding. This has become the front line of control of elections for the Defendants.

This right-wing "ALEC"-type organization named "Election Center" started by voting machine companies and now a staple for election officials who support the corruptible voting machines (to which the Director of Wisconsin's GAB Kevin Kennedy is affiliated);
http://docs.google.com/viewer?a=v&q=cache:wT7Hd9MFK68J:
www.bradblog.com/Docs/ElectionCenter_beverly%2520hills%252
02005%2520agenda5-25.doc+Election+Center&hl=en&gl=us&pid
=bl&srcid=ADGEESgQ1_VQzya02tc-9YWsn_mBqLvZW7BaEAIkbU-
2-dwo2pH-

For more information on the Election Center, and testimony on the history of election fraud in the US, contact:
Brad Friedman, award-winning journalist on election integrity for over 10 years.
www.bradblog.com
brad@bradblog.com

****

Legislative Fraud
ALEC: A creation of the Koch Brothers, this far right arm of the cartel writes the downloadable templates being used in Wisconsin today as the "budget." Almost all of the Wisconsin Republican senators are members, and their membership fees are paid for the state taxpayers.
http://www.alecexposed.org/wiki/ALEC_Exposed

No Wisconsin Democrats are members, however, Rep. Mark Pocan (D) has been investigating ALEC for several years.

In March 2011, Bill Cronon, the UW Madison Professor wrote an editorial for the New York Times regarding ALEC and making the connection between Walker and McCarthy. Soon afterward a public records request was filed by a state Republican Party official demanding access to months of messages on his university e-mail account that referred to certain politicized words and names including the governor and a number of legislators. UW Madison

complied but excluded records involving students because they are protected under FERPA. Nothing was found.
http://www.nytimes.com/2011/03/26/us/politics/26professor.html

Perhaps one of the more subtle aspects in legislative fraud is understanding how it has been woven into election fraud for the past decade, slowly and quietly changing the laws and statutes on local levels to support the voting machine companies. Voter suppression acts are passed, gerrymandering of districts in secret without Democratic input takes place, and the corporations' deep ties to the Republican Party who are buying the votes take more control.

For example, there is much in the Wisconsin statutes about prosecuting voter fraud, but nothing clearly defines the process to hold those engaged in election fraud accountable. GAB employees are not required to communicate with the public about complaints or if an investigation is even going on. The Director consistently uses his language and his power to make decisions to protect the voting machine companies. And now we know, he also has no oversight, as he has withheld complaints against him from the Board.

Legislative fraud was blatant in this session as Republicans intentionally agreed to vote in favor of corporate needs, thus abandoning their constituents and abusing of their majority power. Republicans cut funding to poor districts, increased funding to wealthy constituents, passed "laws" that violated our Constitutional rights of Free Speech and the Right To Assembly, arrested people in violation of their Constitutional rights, enacted legislation to funnel public funds into private black box accounts, cut programs that were not costing the state, supported legislation to make it more difficult for smaller independent businesses to operate, and closed down loan programs for vendors of bigger business that, again, did not cost the state anything. The list is too long and extensive to include in this complaint.

They also are allowing the mining companies to write the legislation for mining that is stripping all protections for people and environment. Walker has also basically dismantled the Department of Natural Resources, leaving the mining companies without any responsibility for the environmental damage they will do (past records indicate the likelihood is high they will do to Wisconsin what they have done everywhere else).

The only way to understand how this session was fraudulent was to listen to the testimony, which I did for hours, or talk to any of the Democrats who had to defend our Democracy against this takeover. I heard for myself how the Republicans accepted no amendments, engaged in very little discussion and passed bill after bill to benefit the mining, trucking, and corporate donors to their campaigns at the expense of the good citizens of the state. Then the propaganda machine cranked out the media fraud claiming we were "union thugs" and were bused in from "out of state." It's true people came from all over the country to help us, but the majority of protesters were there because they knew this hostile takeover of the State was going on, and as lovers of Democracy and Wisconsin, stood up to protect her.

When you consider how election fraud works, legislators, believing that the corporation will rig the votes to get them back in office no longer have to even work. Their behavior, drunk on power, becomes blatantly apparent, which is what I believe was the downfall of the Wisconsin Defendants. Many legislators in both the Assembly and the Senate stand on record to document this. In a speech on the Assembly floor in March, Rep. Therese Berceau said she had been in government for 22 years and had never seen the like of their behavior. She equated the Republicans to zombies, just following along with what they were told to do.[94]

In Wisconsin, legislative sessions are recorded and archived. Any of the following Wisconsin Senators and Representatives can relate the evidence of collusion on the part of the Wisconsin Republicans to purposefully pass legislation to bankrupt the State:.

Senator Jon Erpenbach
8 South, State Capitol
P.O. Box 7882
Madison, WI 53707-7882
608.266.6670 or toll-free 888.549.0027
Fax: 608.266.2508
Sen.Erpenbach@legis.wi.gov

Senator Lena Taylor
415 South, State Capitol
P.O. Box 7882
Madison, WI 53707-7882
Phone: 608.266.5810
FAX: 608.267.2353
Sen.Taylor@legis.wi.gov

Representative Peter Barca
Room 201 West
P.O. Box 8952
Madison, WI 53708
608.266.5504
Rep.Barca@legis.wisconsin.gov

Representative Mark Pocan
Room 309 East
PO Box 8953
Madison, WI 53708
608.266.8570
Rep.Pocan@legis.wisconsin.gov

94 http://www.youtube.com/watch?v=mnwK4LzCoGc

Proof of Violations of Our Free Speech, Freedom of Assembly, and Open Meetings

For an incredible library of documentation of the Defendants' violating our Constitutional rights of Free Speech and Assembly, and Wisconsin's open meeting laws, contact Jeremy Ryan. This young man has stood guard over our Capitol for months, unafraid of arrest, as month after month the Defendants' attempted to remove him, sometimes just for sitting quietly holding a Constitution. He is also the target of an intense hate campaign. For me, he is a patriot of the highest order and because of his constant vigilance to protect this State he should receive a Medal of Bravery.

Jeremy Ryan
Defending Wisconsin
jryan_winston@yahoo.com
http://www.defendingwisconsin.org

****

Judicial Fraud

The history of judicial influence over the past ten years is obvious and enormous. The 2000 election that was decided with a Supreme Court stacked by the Republicans; Citizens United opened the door for the next level of takeover; and in April 2011, Wisconsin's own David Prosser, the Republican judge who was declared the "winner" in the recount in the face of unprecedented evidence of possible fraud, went on to overturn turn Judge Sumi's March court decision that the Republicans did violate Wisconsin's Open Meeting Law when they passed the budget bill in the middle of the night, with no warning, locking out the public, with the Democrats still out of state and only Rep. Peter Barca remaining to try to hold them accountable.
http://www.youtube.com/watch?v=rUA1DJIJOZs

Even Prosser's fellow judges knew the election was rigged to get him on the bench to make the ruling. The shocking minority opinion of the court bluntly and directly accused the majority of fudging the facts to reach the decision they had already determined they wanted to reach. The minority opinion further alleged that the majority was driven by political motives rather than the desire to deliver a fair and judicious opinion:
http://www.forbes.com/sites/rickungar/2011/06/15/the-wisconsin-supreme-court-crisis-far-more-serious-than-the-ruling-on-walkers-anti-collective-bargaining-law/

Prosser is now the subject of an investigation into allegations that he choked a fellow judge, but he refuses to step down despite demands.
http://www.wxow.com/story/15070852/prosser-rejects-calls-for-him-to-take-leave

Prosser is also receiving funding from the Koch Brothers via private supporters, as he faces yet another case coming before the court

involving accusations against the Tea Party. He is refusing to recluse himself and claims he will remain impartial. None of us believes this.
http://www.jsonline.com/news/statepolitics/127662258.html

Prosser's former assistant Kathy Nickolaus is now county clerk of Waukesha, where there have been routine disruptions and obstructions to transparent elections, including the outcome of the recall election of August 9 in a highly contested race that the Republicans needed to win. At the time of writing this letter, Nickolaus is under investigation for fraud from the Supreme Court recount, but was still allowed to be in charge of the ballots for several wards in the most important recall for the Republicans, Alberta Darling in the 8th, head of the Joint Finance Committee and she remains in a very powerful position.

Initial examination of the results clearly shows the pattern that appears in election tampering: the exact flip of the percentages late in the day:
http://myplayfulself.com/wordpress/

****

Media Fraud
Without the help of right-wing media, this takeover could not be possible. It is not difficult to prove fraud here as many Comedy Central pundits have produced reports comparing what Fox claims to what really happened. It is no less true in Wisconsin and we have clear documentation and evidence:

Fox News substitutes footage of California—purposefully misleading the public and misrepresenting our Wisconsin peaceful protests as being violent:
http://www.youtube.com/watch?v=aOzerRfB27o

Another broadcast from Fox is intentionally manipulated to broadcast media fraud with claims of an assault:
http://www.youtube.com/watch?v=GHB7_d5-twg

Fox News' Rupert Murdoch on trial for illegal activities, including hacking into the phone message of a victim of 9/11:
http://www.huffingtonpost.com/2011/07/14/fbi-news-corp-investigation_n_898653.html

MacIver Institute continues to campaign for Walker despite its 501(c)(3) organization listing making it illegal for them to do so.
http://wcmcoop.com/members/maciver-institute-and-afp-working-for-walker-campaign/

Cyberwarriors
Another media strategy has been to use cyberwarriors, people trained to hit online media sites for the sole purpose of spreading lies, causing confusion by attacking legitimate members, reporting

legitimate posts as spam to get them banned, as well as responding to news articles and blog posts with hatred and dissent:

GOP pays for & trains Tea Party activists in guerrilla Internet tactics to "Control the Online Dialogue
http://current.com/community/93149403_gop-busted-paying-for-training-tea-party-activists-in-guerilla-internet-tactics-control-the-online-dialogue.htm

ATTACHMENT TWO
Illegal Activities, Legislative Fraud, Proof of Intent and Collusion on the part of Wisconsin Republicans

2009: Even before he took office as governor, Scott Walker unveils his martial law plans in Milwaukee.
http://www.youtube.com/watch?v=HSR7ZG-fcjQ

December 2010: Wisconsin financials show the State is actually in the black at the end of the year until Walker gives tax breaks to some out-of-state corporations right out of the gate to put us in the hole.
http://thepoliticalenvironment.blogspot.com/2011/02/calling-all-media-wisconsin-in-january.html

February 1: Democrats read the horror of the budget bill and leave the state as a filibuster in order to give us time to read it. We are mortified.
http://www.mercatornet.com/sheila_liaugminas/view/8712/

February 18: Republicans citizens who voted for this crop of senators will testify that they were lied to.
http://www.theawl.com/2011/03/a-blueprint-for-a-takeover-wisconsin-Republicans-lied-while-the-kochs-schemed

February 25: Wisconsin Assembly is hit with the same bad behavior from Assembly Republicans when they start voting early and end before the entire roll call is taken.
http://wwwwakeupamericans-spree.blogspot.com/2011/02/wi-assembly-passes-controversial-walker.html

February 27 & March 2: Walker illegally shuts down the Capitol and gets his first restraining order which he promptly ignores and later ignores the second one too.
http://crooksandliars.com/nicole-belle/thousands-crowd-wisconsin-state-capit
http://www.peoplesworld.org/walker-ignores-court-order-locks-out-wisconsin-protesters/

March 1: Democrats are not allowed into the Capitol building unless they show Capitol ID and no one else is allowed in.
http://www.youtube.com/watch?v=H5SIyYzmJSU

March 2: Even former Congressman Obey is denied access to his meeting inside.
http://www.youtube.com/watch?v=KwwtvrH0Vn8

March 3: Democrats bring their offices outside to reach their constituents.
http://tpmdc.talkingpointsmemo.com/2011/03/wisconsin-assembly-dems-set-up-office-outside-protesting-capitol-restrictions.php

March 8: Walker claims unions have budgetary impact.
http://walker.wi.gov/journal_media_detail.asp?prid=5675&locid=177

March 9: Republicans remove the union busting measures from the budget bill and try to pass it while violating open meeting laws. Rep. Barca was left holding the proof of this illegal act, and tried to call them on it.
http://www.thedailypage.com/daily/article.php?article=32693

March 18: Judge Sumi issues restraining order to stop the publication of the budget bill.
http://www.redstate.com/lineholder/2011/03/18/wi-judge-sumi-issues-temporary-restraining-order-on-act-10/

March 28: Republicans illegally publish their illegal bill anyway again breaking the law.
http://blogs.forbes.com/rickungar/2011/03/28/walker-ignores-court-order-begins-enforcement-of-anti-collective-bargaining-law/

April 11: Walker's supporter William Gardner, president and chief executive officer of Wisconsin & Southern Railroad Co., charged with funneling $60,000 to Walker through his employees and ends up with $166,000 fine.
http://www.jsonline.com/news/statepolitics/119595644.html

May 5: Republicans hire out-of-state right-wingers to collect names illegally for Democrat recall petitions.
http://www.wisDemocrats.org/news/press/view/2011-05-gop-election-fraud-exposed

May 19: Republicans pass a voter suppression law that outright keeps voters from the polls and was rammed through the legislature.
http://www.progressive.org/kemble051911.html

May 25: Republicans pass Voter Suppression Bill and election integrity activists considering suing.
http://www.jsonline.com/news/statepolitics/122588869.html

May 26: Dane County Court rules Republicans violated open meeting laws.
http://www.newser.com/story/119519/judge-strikes-down-wisconsins-anti-union-law.html

June 2: A recording documenting the Republicans making the plan to run the fake candidates in violation of the law.
http://www.politicususa.com/en/secret-tape-wisconsin-gop

June 27: Prosser is accused by Justice Ann Walsh Bradley of choking her and an investigation begins.
http://www.politico.com/news/stories/0611/57835.html

July 12: Right to Life Robo Calls to Democratic voters, with intent to cause confusion.
http://www.wisn.com/r/28525033/detail.html

July 12: Republicans run "fake Democrats" with the sole intention to tamper with the date and results of the primary recall elections, thereby committing perjury, as in order to collect support signatures, they had to swear they would work for the Democratic Party goals. Wisconsin statute 12.13(3)(a) says, "No person may file a declaration of candidacy 'knowing any part is falsely made.' If a candidate claims to support a party he or she does not actually support, that candidate is in violation of 12.13(3)(a)." Cost to State: $400,000.
http://www.chicagotribune.com/news/local/breaking/chi-fake-Democrats-run-in-wisconsin-primaries-for-recall-elections-20110712,0,1287204.story

July 21: With no input from Democrats, Republicans engage in gerrymandering by redistricting using $395/hour attorneys at taxpayer expense to draw up secret maps. [Republicans force party members to sign secrecy agreements that also impel them to ignore the public comments.]
http://www.jsonline.mobi/more/news/wisconsin/125988098.htm
[http://www.jsonline.com/news/statepolitics/lawmakers-were-made-to-pledge-secrecy-over-redistricting-9643ep0-138826854.html]

July 27: Republicans threaten to close DMVs in Democratic districts where IDs necessary for voting can be obtained.
http://neweranews.org/blog/gov-walker-wants-to-close-dmvs-in-Democratic-districts-not-a-fan-of-Democracy

July 27: Voter Suppression Law creates confusion at the DMV on obtaining voter ID card. Women is told there is not enough activity on her son' bank account to obtain ID.
http://www.disinfo.com/2011/07/bank-activity-required-for-wisconsin-voter-id/

August 1: Americans for Prosperity, the Wisconsin Tea Party, Wisconsin Family Action PAC, and United Sportsmen of Wisconsin collude to send out fraudulent information in mailers targeting Democrats with the intent to mislead and tamper with votes.
http://www.jsonline.com/blogs/news/126530753.html?page=4

August 4: Complaint filed against Sen. Alberta Darling for multiple felonies as part of a collusion and obstruction conspiracy.
http://www.wisDemocrats.org/news/press/view/2011-08-alberta-darlings-illegal-coverup

August 8: Government "Accountability" Board admits in e-mails that they censor information being sent to Board Members.
https://docs.google.com/document/d/1mAmzXG5nHp97nYUlVpGySnbdfRZq_7eFOBU9F5o03CU/edit?hl=en_US

August 9: Clerks create confusion on Election Day by closing polling places and providing confusing information.
http://www.politiscoop.com/component/content/article/35-last-24h-news/452-voters-disenfranchisedin-glendale.html

August 18: Walker declares he will eliminate Secretary of State, Attorney General and Treasurer, giving him more unprecedented power to control and access millions of dollars of public trust money.
http://www.progressive.org/Republicans_partisan_agenda.html

Ballot bag after ballot bag, sealed so poorly that one could unroll the opening and remove and add ballots as needed. These Waukesha bags were among over 800 anomalies documented by observers and ignored by the Government Accountability Board.

Manifesto of the Destiny of World Peace

We the People acknowledge that our infinite spirit has been gifted with the creative life force of both humanity and divinity. We now stand and state our full intention to channel that life force into the manifestation of world peace. We invite all citizens to join with us in this declaration of a Manifesto of the Destiny of World Peace.

We intend to create into physical form a family of humankind residing on Earth who see past the illusions of fear, and using conscious commitment to self-love and civic responsibility, transform the fear-based infrastructure to a love-based one.

With our human and divine heart and mind, our physical body and infinite spirit, we begin by staking a claim of complete self-responsibility to all of the energy within our domain. From this commitment to our own peace, we bring peace to all levels of creation that are within our jurisdiction.

We commit to peace within relationships between husband and wife, parent and child, governed and government, master and servant, neighbor and neighbor, tribe and tribe, with our own selves. We commit to infuse every relationship—individual and collective—with decisions made for the good of all involved, thereby supporting a love-based infrastructure within those relationships.

We agree to accept responsibility for all decisions that we make, and to inspire through example to educate others.

We believe that it is our destiny to manifest this peace, and that because it is destiny, there will be no obstacle or challenge too great to prevent the actualization of this destiny. We commit to using the elements of every human challenge, no matter how destructive in nature they appear to be, to take action for the good of the whole.

We agree that all generations that have come before and all that will come after have peace as their birthright; not as an award to be earned, but a grace granted by the truth of our spiritual essence. We intend to work for the future generations, so that they may be born into a love-based infrastructure.

Lastly, we fully intend to persist with this movement until peace is achieved on a global level.

I, the undersigned, agree this _____ day of __________________

____

your name

Barbara With is an international peace activist, award-winning author, composer, performer, psychic, workshop facilitator and inspirational speaker living on Madeline Island, Wisconsin. Her other books include *Imagining Einstein: Essays on M-Theory, World Peace & The Science of Compassion*, *Party of Twelve: The Afterlife Interviews*, *Party of Twelve: Post 9/11*, *Diaries of a Psychic Sorority* and *Guerrilla Publishing: How To Become a Published Author For Less Than $1500 & Keep 100% Of The Profits*.

She is a founding member of the Wisconsin Citizens Media Coop and reports regularly on the events in Wisconsin. She has also researched and developed Conflict REVOLUTION®, a revolutionary new way to approach conflict, and conducts workshops around the world. She has two CDs of original music, *Innocent Future* and *Solitaire*.

www.barbarawith.com
www.wcmcoop.com

www.ingramcontent.com/pod-product-compliance
Lightning Source LLC
Chambersburg PA
CBHW021835020426
42334CB00014B/636
* 9 7 8 0 9 6 6 1 3 7 8 2 8 *